Letters to a Beekeeper

Steve Benbow

Letters to a Beekeeper

Alys Fowler

Unbound

This edition first published in 2017

Unbound
6th Floor Mutual House
70 Conduit Street
London W1S 2GF
www.unbound.com

Steve's bee image © Patrick Guenette
Alys's flower image © nicoolay
Bee illustrations © Chris Shields
Tintype images, pp. 38 & 44 © Tif Hunter
Mr Holmes photograph, p. 147 © Photo 12 / Alamy Stock Photo
All other photographs © Steve J. Benbow

Designed by Holmes Wood

A CIP record for this book is available from the British Library

ISBN 978-1-78352-115-9 (trade hbk)
ISBN 978-1-78352-165-4 (ebook)
ISBN 978-1-78352-116-6 (limited edition)

Printed in Italy by L.E.G.O. S.p.A.

This book is dedicated to all those
who plant the seeds
that feed the bees

Dear Reader,

The book you are holding came about in a rather different way to most others. It was funded directly by readers through a new website: Unbound. Unbound is the creation of three writers. We started the company because we believed there had to be a better deal for both writers and readers. On the Unbound website, authors share the ideas for the books they want to write directly with readers. If enough of you support the book by pledging for it in advance, we produce a beautifully bound special subscribers' edition and distribute a regular edition and e-book wherever books are sold, in shops and online.

This new way of publishing is actually a very old idea (Samuel Johnson funded his dictionary this way). We're just using the internet to build each writer a network of patrons. At the back of this book, you'll find the names of all the people who made it happen.

Publishing in this way means readers are no longer just passive consumers of the books they buy, and authors are free to write the books they really want. They get a much fairer return too – half the profits their books generate, rather than a tiny percentage of the cover price.

If you're not yet a subscriber, we hope that you'll want to join our publishing revolution and have your name listed in one of our books in the future. To get you started, here is a £5 discount on your first pledge. Just visit unbound.com, make your pledge and type BEEKEEPER in the promo code box when you check out.

Thank you for your support,

Dan, Justin and John
Founders, Unbound

CONTENTS

...

Beginning

Steve Benbow

Alys Fowler

I don't know who was responsible for getting us together in the first place – the wildly independent gardener and lover of damp tweed, goat wool socks and small dogs with the destitute vagrant and nomadic beekeeper. It could have been an enthusiastic press officer or a literary festival organiser, but however it happened, we found ourselves speaking at the Edinburgh Festival together, promoting our new books. To whoever it was, I would like to say: 'It was a bold, inspired arranged marriage.'

If you look at the photographs taken that day, I'm clean shaven and coiffed. It had been the first night I'd slept in a bed for almost two years, not only that, but it was a king-size with six pillows and crisp starched sheets. For the first time in a long time, I was not looking, as my grandfather used to say, 'like I'd been pulled through a hedge backwards'.

We knew very little about each other. While I had taken advantage of free overnight accommodation, Alys was jetting in from Brum for the day. We met for a light lunch at The Dogs on Hanover Street, to go over the running order before our event. I was giving out jars of honey as a way of an introduction and perhaps also to show how marvellous my bees were at producing delicious stuff. Alys, with delicate beads of coral and tumbling hair of a similar colour, appeared delighted with my offerings – or she was just very polite about my bumbling nervousness.

Later that day, on stage in the venue's giant felt yurts, Alys positioned herself as the lone centre forward, skilfully weaving through the audience's tricky questioning with ease. Me, well, I was the clumsy, shy defender, hands in pockets, fumbling around the halfway line, getting flustered when the ball was booted in my direction.

But as I stood and listened from the side of the stage, I realised how incredible her horticultural knowledge was. She seemed to understand everything that lay in the ground and sprouted, shooted, budded, flowered and fruited. I wondered what she knew about bees – if she'd ever considered keeping them?

She was cautious when I asked her: she was well aware they required a huge amount of commitment and vigilance. But she'd been a country girl once, kept chickens and, like me, spent the majority of her days working the land.

Back in London, homeless and quite destitute, my ingenious and resourceful bees were my only real form of income. They gave me food for the table and a roof over my head, albeit a cold, damp warehouse in Bermondsey with asbestos sheeting. But it was all provided by the sale of their incredible honey. In a very crude and essential way, my bees were keeping the wolf from the door.

I had made a conscious decision not to get a flat when I moved back into town but to prioritise somewhere for my hives and equipment to be stored. I slept rough around the bee sites I had, either by camping or bedding down on the floor of my van. Then in the sodden roof space cavity of the vast warehouse, I would curl up like a dog, hoping that no one disturbed me.

My bees had always managed to flourish in the city, from the first day I brought them to the capital almost twenty years ago, in the back of my neon-green VW Golf. They were immense grafters from the off, a bit like me, able to scratch a living from what was around them and in their case, finding good extensive forage, in the most unlikely of settings.

The Bees installation at the Tate was the brainchild of one of the directors who had heard about my bees on London rooftops and recruited my services. At Tate Britain apiary, the bees foraged on the gigantic lime trees and fantastic vigorous nectar-yielding trees, aptly named 'Trees of Heaven'. These both produce the most aromatic nectar from mid June for about three to four weeks and if the weather conditions are right, a bumper harvest for all.

However, it is the early season pollen my critters crave at key stages of the colony's expansion. As the days become longer and the temperatures stabilise, the brood nest requires pollen for grub and larvae development and I had always loved the idea of a fast food pit-stop right below where they live, to keep them topped up with treats and gems for their expansion.

The original Tate art gallery was established by a chap who ironically made his living from another sweet substance – sugar. In the centre of the complex is the staff garden, a strip of oblong land about the size of a five-a-side football pitch. Dozens of lichen-covered park benches surround this popular strip, which conveniently receives a good lashing of sun from lunchtime onwards. That was the site I wanted for my bug diner: a pollinator paradise in the middle of the city. Not some manicured rose garden or artificial turfed lawn with box hedging, but solitude for all that grazed there. But my knowledge was limited; I didn't have the expertise to build the wilderness.

I remember the first call I put in to Alys after the event. It was a bright winter's morning and I had opened the roller shutter in my warehouse in Bermondsey to let in some daylight. That's when I popped the question: 'Would you… help build a garden for my bees, please?' It took very little persuasion. Honey was exchanged. And then Alys's side of the bargain: that I would help her build her own hive. Could this work? Two strong personalities coming together to trade skills and build something quite remarkable. My beekeeping knowledge in exchange for her wisdom of plants. A wonderful collaboration, resulting in a greater richness of nectar for the capital's pollinators. What could go wrong?

'My beekeeping knowledge in exchange for her wisdom of plants'

STEVE'S THOUGHTS…

He likes bees and I like flowers. It's a perfect match, right? He was a beekeeper, a man who knew his trees by their flowers and chased an endless summer. I was always going to fall for that. He got me hooked on his honey and before I knew it, I was agreeing to help him build a garden. You can't say that Steve is anything other than persuasive.

When the honeycomb was all but consumed, when we had drunk beer and tea and swapped eggs and turnips and greens for more honey, once the tender beginnings of friendship were spun and we started to share details and learned how to amuse each other, we set about a plan for this book. On reflection, for me, it was just a ruse to keep up the friendship, an elaborate one I'll admit, but how else do you keep hold of a wandering man? The plan was sometimes fanciful and wildly impractical: Steve wanted me to follow behind his Massey Ferguson tractor on my bike from Shropshire to London and then plough up as many lawns as we could (neither of us can plough). He suggested we get a narrow boat and float to London, sowing seeds along the way.

And eventually we settled upon one that seemed to make sense. I would help Steve's bees, and for that matter any other pollinators hanging around Tate Britain, by sowing a wild garden full of flowers that he could learn to garden in.

Honey is a hard-earned sort of gold: it requires a lot of work from the bees and from the keeper too. It is a precious resource that shouldn't be squandered. But bees want something back in return for their work – usually dinner, in the form of nectar or pollen, though some bees use plants merely for sex, either as a sort of motel or as a place to pick up cologne.

Bees are easily exploited and we all know what a hard time they are having – if you want to help them out, then you have to offer a fine spread. In simple terms, the more plants you add to your garden the more bees you can feed. I was going to help Steve build an urban garden for all the bees in town.

In return, Steve would give me my first beehive stocked full of gentle bees. It seemed a very good division of labour and would hopefully teach us both about how our worlds interacted, how they were threaded together, despite us being in different cities.

This is the story of how I got my first swarm; of a little land we borrowed from Tate Britain to make a wildflower patch for all the bees in town; of the letters, postcards, texts and packages that we sent; and of the adventures we went on.

It's the story of how I went from a curious onlooker to committed beekeeper and Steve from a bee-obsessed nomad to a collector of seeds, a waterer and even a weeder. And it's the story of our friendship, which survived weeds, swarms and dry soil, to eventually blossom and thrive.

ALYS'S THOUGHTS...

Dear Alys.

29th October   -16 degrees C bright blue
sky and the bees are dashing in with bright
orange pollen still from the ivy and seem
oblivious to the carnage around them,
after the mighty storm which raged
last night.

It would seem the parapit which
surrounds the small young Paksshine
hives on the roof protected them
from the gails — along with the brick
on each roof.

However I decided to go and check all the other
hives around the Capital at Tate Mod/Brit
and bartnums to check that they
were all upright and
safe this
morning.

There were huge branches down everywhere as I
drove to each site and I was expecting the
worst. At Lambeth Bridge at the
back of the Palace there was a huge
limb which had been wrenched of
a giant Acacia – red chequered
tape surrounded it like a crime
scene.

I need not to have worried mind
you all the hives were upright
and intact. The bricks had
done their job again, keeping
the roofs on Snug.

Please excuse the writing
paper its 1.36am and I just
thought I would drop you a note
and rip open an envelope –
Clearly very badly.

I hope your garden did not
take the battering the South took
Clearly we have lost some valued cedar
sources overnight here.
So Garden at Tate
must crack on Soon.
Running out of room
Yours the
beekeeper

14th December

Dearest Ben,

I've spent all day waiting for the scaffolders to come and take down their poles etc. I've been pacing up and down the house like some caged animal. Every two seconds back to the garden and then to the front door (I missed them the last time). And here between stretches I saw her, a great huge fat Bombus terrestris queen, so large that you'd hardly believe she could fly.

Buff-tails are supposed to be very fond of Arbutus unedo, the strawberry tree. It flowers from now into December, tiny white bells like bell heather, and if the weather is mild are often followed by the strawberry-like fruit.

The species name unedo - means 'eat only once' as Pliny thought them tasteless.

In Spain the fruit are fermented into an alcoholic concoction that I always fantasize I'll make one day.

Still it's very pleasing to find her humming on my tree.

I chased her around the garden only to hear the stragglers knocking and thus had to leave her be.

I love those fat queens, how can something so heavy fly? She defies logic. I hope she comes back again soon.

Now that the straggling is gone I am off to plant yet more bulbs.

Speak soon,

Dylan

17th December

Dearest Steve

Firstly here is your christmas present. Socks made from goats! These truly are the best socks in the world; warm, hard wearing and ready for an adventure if you so wish...

I finally finished planting out the very last of the bulbs. A small smattering of dwarf daffodil 'Minnow' around the base of the allotment bench. It's a tiny, highly fragrant yellow daff to please anyone who wants to rest.

Down where the bees shall live I have planted so many bulbs that palms had blisters. Hundreds upon hundreds of crocus, muscari, chionodoxa, mixed dwarf fox daffodil and scillas. A smorgasbord of early pollen for the welsh darlings and any other flying bumble or worthy fruit bender to come out.

I also planted several rows of tulips
on my plot. I feel conflicted by
this act. I love picking tulips for
indoors. I love the way a tulip
opens, its blatant, almost indecent
unfurling and then its demise.
I think a tulip almost looks best when
going over. But I also know that
unless the tulip package specifically
states that it is pesticide free, you can
bet that it has been drenched in pesticides.
Otherwise how do those endless rows
of tulips remain unblemished by
aphids or slug or greenfly?

  I tell myself that as long as I
pick them before they opened —
pays no pollinator gets inside it is
somehow alright. But let's face it
this is hardly fine. The bulbs will
release pesticides into the soil to permit
the plant to come.

'A smorgasboard
of early pollen for
the welsh darling
and any other flying
bumble or hoverfly
that decide to
come out'

Still throwing all the bulbs into landfill isn't much of an alternative. It is something that needs addressing though. So much of cheap horticulture, bedding plants, bulbs, pot grown shrubs etc are drenched in neo-nic and other chemicals. Yet we all bang on about planting for pollinators and possibly much of what people plant out of goodwill is a ticking time bomb.

Still that's one to tackle next year... right now I have willow to harvest and the sun is shining so I am off out. When we speak next it will be a new year,

do good celebrations and what not and see you the other side.

With love,

A.

The Bees I Have Seen

I am sorry if I have run off half way through a conversation, if I have looked askance or distracted, fallen to my knees to look down a hole or demanded that we stop everything to chase a bee, but once you meet one close up, you want to meet the whole tribe.

Here are some of the bees I've said hello to in the past few summers. If I can find them, anyone can.

MALE OR FEMALE
...

· Females tend to have a pointed bottom, from which their sting appears.
· Males have a flat, rounded bum with no sting (though some solitary males may have spines or pegs).
· Only females carry pollen. This is carried on special hairs called scopa. These can either be on their legs or the underside of their abdomen. The legs have a concave space, which is shiny and fringed with hairs for carrying pollen. Female bumblebees' legs are hairier for this reason.
· Females are busy; they flit around from flower to flower.
· Males sit lazily on flowers and don't collect pollen.
· Males often are dusted with pollen (no need to brush it off). Whereas females will groom the pollen into their pollen baskets/scopas.
· Males get drunk more often (OK that's a bit of a generalisation, but you do sometimes see them drunk on fermenting sugars).
· Males often have moustaches. These 'taches outdo any hipster, for what it's worth.
· Males often have yellow faces.
· Males have long, distinctive antennae that are curved.
· Females have an elbow in the antennae.

ALYS'S THOUGHTS...

26

BUMBLEBEES
...

· Bumblebees are social nesters.
· The earliest workers can often
  be small, particularly to type.
· Late in the year bumbles can look
  very worn, often their thorax is rubbed
  bare from all that pollinating. It can
  look quite shiny. This is age rather
  than type.
· Bumbles' colours can fade, so may
  not look true to type.
· They can vary widely within a species.
  It's possible to have more or less colour.
· There are also quite a few other insects
  that have specialised in looking like
  a bumble (hoverflies in particular),
  so remember: four wings, nipped
  in waist is a bee; two wings, no waist
  is a fly.

WHITE-TAILED BUMBLEBEE
Bombus lucorum
(from the Latin *lucus*, meaning
sacred thicket or wood)
...

· Hard to tell the difference between
  the white-tailed and the buff,
  particularly amongst workers.
· All have a yellow collar to the
  thorax, and another yellow band
  on the abdomen. The males have
  a yellow moustache (whereas buff-tails
  have a black moustache). Some males
  have an additional band at the rear
  of the thorax.
· Robust, large, short tongue, very
  common and widespread. If in doubt
  declare it a white-tailed and you are
  probably right.
· Queens are often the first bumbles
  seen in spring.
· On the wing from February
  to October.
· Large nests up to 200 workers.
  Nests mostly underground, always
  under cover. Loves to nectar-rob
  long-tube flowers it can't reach.
  Particularly fond of doing this
  to broad, runner and French beans.
· Spring queens love aphid dews off
  conifers so it's possible to see large
  swarms this way.

ALYS'S THOUGHTS...

BUFF-TAILED BUMBLEBEE
Bombus terrestris
(from the Latin *terra*, of the earth)
...

· Buff-tailed bumbles look much
like white-tailed bumbles, although
their bum is buff-coloured.
However, white-tailed bumbles can
often have discolouration to their tail,
so this is not always a good indicator.
· The queen of the buff-tailed is slightly
smaller than the queen of the white-
tailed. Both emerge in early spring.
· The male buff-tailed bees have
black facial hair as opposed to
yellow on the white-tailed male.
· The nests are of similar size and
location, although buff-tailed like
slightly shadier spots.

GARDEN BUMBLEBEE
Bombus horturum
(from the Latin *hortus*, garden)
...

· This bee has the longest tongue
of the British bumbles and thus
it likes to visit all sorts of flowers
that are out of reach to other
bumbles: honeysuckle, foxgloves,
beans, red clover, anything with
a long flower tube.
· It has a large white tail with yellow
bands to a black body. It has a yellow
band on its collar and at the bottom
of the thorax and the top of the
abdomen. Long face, males with
black moustache. Large, robust
and likes to unfurl its very long
tongue just as it approaches a flower.
· Loves gardens, parks, municipal
hanging baskets and anywhere else
we like to plant flowers.
· Nest often underground, but can
be elsewhere, always under cover.
· On the wing from March to October.
· Nest up to 100 workers.

ALYS'S THOUGHTS...

28

EARLY/MEADOW BUMBLEBEE
Bombus pratorum
(from the Latin *pratum*, of the meadows)
···

· This is a small black bumble with
  yellow bands (one on thorax and
  one on abdomen) and an orange
  bum. It often looks yellow with
  a black band. Male has very distinct
  yellow face moustache and hairs.
· Males can be almost all yellow and
  some workers are almost all black.
  It's a very nimble bumble, happy
  to hang upside down to work a flower
  if necessary. It often likes to hover
  for a bit and then dart and then hover
  again. It can be very furry and at first
  glance you can mistake it for a hoverfly
  flight pattern.
· Likes gardens, loves brambles and
  raspberries, but will happily choose
  a wide range of flowers.
· Colonies of up to 100 individuals.
  Can produce a second generation
  of nest if the weather is good.
  Usually, however, over by
  mid-summer.
· On the wing, first generation
  April to June, second generation
  June to October.
· Nest above and below ground,
  will use bird boxes.
· Queen overwinters in the ground.

COMMON CARDER
Bombus pascuorum
···

· If I were a bee, I'd be this one.
  The queens, workers and males
  are all pale ginger-brown with
  very shaggy hair. They can have
  lots of black hairs on their bum,
  particularly if they are from the
  south. Their colour fades considerably
  over the summer (oh, do I understand
  that one).
· The males have ginger moustaches.
· This is a medium sized bee with
  a pleasingly round bum (slightly more
  ovoid in males) and a long tongue.
· Loves gardens, dead nettles and
  Lamium species, beans and
  foxgloves too.
· It is one of the first carders to be seen
  in spring.
· Tends to nest in the ground and the
  bees collect moss to cover the entrance
  of the nest. Very mild-tempered,
  up to 100 individuals per nest.
· On the wing from June to November.

ALYS'S THOUGHTS...

RED-TAILED BUMBLEBEE
LARGE RED-TAILED BUMBLEBEE
Bombus lapidarius
...

· A common southern species with
a big red bum. There are two basic
variations: the queen, workers and
males can have a yellow collar, some
males can have a bright yellow face
and some can be all black with a red
bum. The antennae are short and the
pollen-basket hairs on workers are
very long and black.
· The queen emerges early spring and
likes to nest just below the ground.
Colonies can be large, over 150.
Interestingly, newly mated queens
often hibernate together in north-
facing banks and woodlands.
· Likes gardens, woodland glades,
grasslands and messy edges.
· Likes yellow flowers, scabious
and any knapweed.
· The males are often very active
and can be seen patrolling around
bushes and hedge lines.
· On the wing from March to October.

TREE BUMBLEBEE
...

· Recent import from France, first
appeared in 2001.
· Very obvious marking, bright ginger
thorax, black abdomen and white bum.
· Large colonies, somewhat noisy, males
love to hang out in gangs doing figure
eights outside the entrance of a nest
in hope of impressing a young,
emerging queen.
· Males smaller than females.
· Only time I have ever seen
a queen being mated was this
species. She was so uninterested
that she continued feeding whilst
the male clung on for dear life.
· Loves nesting up high in trees, bird
boxes, your attic and my roof space.
· Peak activity from late May
to early June.

ALYS'S THOUGHTS...

SOLITARY BEES
...

HAIRY-FOOTED FLOWER BEE
Anthophora plumipes
...

- Females appear first and are easy
  to spot because they are all black
  and fly faster than any other bee.
- They always appear in early spring.
- They often stick their tongue out
  when they fly.
- Absolutely obsessed with Pulmonaria,
  Comfrey and any other lungwort.
- Males rather dull brown with a dark
  tail. They are often the first bees
  of the year to emerge. Cream-coloured
  face (no bumblebee has this). Often
  hover in front of the flower and when
  pursuing females.
- Nests in soft mortar, old cobs walls
  and sometime the ground, like bare,
  compacted clay soil.
- Urban bee, doesn't mind built-up
  areas, as long as there are lungworts.

TAWNY MINING BEE
Andrena fulva
...

- Lovely, spring-flying little bee.
  The female is bright orangey-brown
  with a black face and legs, distinctly
  cute-looking bee, very hairy. The male
  is slimmer, less densely orangey-brown
  and has a very big white 'tache.
- On the wing from early April to June
  and the males appear first.
- The nests are tiny holes in the ground
  surrounded by a volcano-like mound
  of excavated soil. Loves to nest
  in lawns, flowerbeds, mown banks,
  roadside verges, and field margins.
- Loves everything from weeds
  to garden and fruit flowers such
  as cherry, apples and pears.
  Very important fruit pollinator.
  Thank this bee for your apples.
- Non-aggressive.

ALYS'S THOUGHTS...

ASHY MINING BEE
Andrena cineraria
...

· Early spring-flying bee, it's a black bee, with a glossy blue-black bum and two broad, ashy-white bands to the top and bottom of the thorax. The males have a distinctive tuft of white, large moustache. Although solitary, they often nest in dense bee cities. Loves nesting in short turf and lawns, where it makes a tiny nest surrounded by a volcano of soil spoil. Common in parks, gardens, roadside verges, orchards and cropped field margins.
· Flies from March to mid-June.
· Loves foraging on everything, from weeds to apples.
· Non-aggressive.

WOOL-CARDER BEE
Anthidium manicatum
...

· Largest of the solitary bees. Males are larger than females, though both look similar. Dark-black abdomen with a pattern of yellow spots, pale hairs to black thorax, distinct yellow markings on the face.
· Easy to spot the males because they are very territorial to a favourite foraging spot or plant. Will chase other bees off if necessary. Only females are allowed to visit their flowers and it's at these sites that mating takes place.
· Males have a series of stout spines around their abdomen that they often use if they feel threatened or if their space is being invaded.
· Females collect pollen on the underside of their abdomen.
· Loves nesting in hollow stems, crevices in mortar joints, burrows in soil, dead wood and various man-made objects.
· The female has special mandibles (mouthparts) that allow her to collect fine hairs of plants (particularly lamb's ears, verbascum, cobweb houseleeks, yarrow and cotton thistle – plant these and after time you'll get wool carders).
· These hairs are then teased out using her mandibles to line the nest and then tamped down with her bum. Teasing the plant hairs is similar to carding in wool-making, hence her name.
· Flies from late May to early August.

ALYS'S THOUGHTS...

IVY BEE
Collete hederae
...

· Loves ivy pollen. Recent introduction from southern Europe (actually only known to science for about the last thirty years).
· Males emerge first.
· Furry orange thorax (much more so than a honey bee), bands of pale yellow and black on abdomen. Simply identified because if its collecting pollen from ivy, it's mostly likely to be an ivy bee.
· On the wing from early September to early November.
· Peak activity seen late in the year when ivy is in flower.
· Loves nesting in loose soil in bee cities, up to 10,000 per nest.
· Loves lawns, short turf and south-facing banks.
· Males often seen seemingly swarming low on the ground, but actually just looking for females.
· Loves orgies. Mates in a bizarre nest ball that rolls about – kind of needs to be seen to be believed.
· Can sting, but only if you decide to squeeze it between your finger and thumb.

CAVITY NESTING BEES
...

· Solitary nesters in aerial locations such as borings in wood, hollow dead stems of plants and mortar.
· Many collect pollen underneath their abdomen rather than on their legs. If you see a bee with pollen on its belly, it's bound to be a cavity nester.

HAREBELL CARPENTER BEE
Chlostoma campanularum
...

· I've only found this in other people's gardens, unsurprisingly on bellflowers, *Campanula* species, their favourite flowers.
· Predominately black bee, small, narrow and cylindrical in shape.
· Females have distinct pale scopa hairs on underbelly, males have none.
· Males have two pronged pegs that stick out of their bum which allows them to cling to the inside of the flower, overnight if necessary, if the weather is too poor to fly.
· Mating takes place inside *Campanula* flowers.
· Found in gardens, urban or rural; not found in Wales or Scotland though.
· Nests in small bore beetle burrows, loves woodworm-infested wood and dried reed stems, in rotting sheds, planks or fence posts. Another reason to have a woodpile (or a rotting shed).
· Flies from mid-June to mid-August.

ALYS'S THOUGHTS...

LEAFCUTTER BEE
Megachile species
...

- Not entirely sure I know which species I saw, probably Willughby's leafcutter bee *Megachile willughbiella* as this is the most common.
- This bee looks much like a honeybee, though it is solitary. The underside of the abdomen is bright orange and on females is often covered with pollen. The females have a distinct face with large mouthparts for cutting leaves.
- I first spotted mine excavating a hole in a pot to make a nest. Though they will commonly use existing holes in plants stems, dead wood, old walls and bee hotels. They cut discs out of leaves (they seem to love roses in particular) and glue the leaves together with their saliva to line the inside of their nest. They partition off each cell with a leaf wall and finish off the nest with a final leaf door.
- Flies April to August.

RED MASON BEE
Osmia bicornis
...

- Common spring flying bee, happy in urban environment.
- Flight period from late March to early June.
- Females have two distinct horns and dark hairs over their faces. Their bodies are bright orange and furry.
- Males have white hair on their faces, no pollen scopa and longer antennae.
- Males appear two weeks before females.
- Loves apples, very important wild pollinator of fruit trees and a very effective pollinator, partly because of the pollen scopa on underside of abdomen.
- Loves nesting in cavities, particularly in old mortar.
- Nests are linear, each cell is partitioned off with mud, which doubles as the back of the next cell. She closes the nest off with a final plug of mud and then heads off to seek a new nest location. If you are lucky, you can hear the female chewing.
- I have several nesting in my airbricks in my office and many in artificial nests that I've put out. Artificial nests must face south, be one metre above ground and be relatively near water and mud.

ALYS'S THOUGHTS...

BLUE MASON BEE
Osmia caerulescens
...

· Small, bluish-black bees with striped,
pale bands to abdomen. Can have
an orange tinge to the thorax
when young. Female carries pollen
on underside and can be seen with
a ball of mashed-up plant material
for nest.
· Nest uses existing cavities in dead
wood, crevices in masonry and
bee hotels. Each cell is portioned
off and closed with a partition
of masticated leaf material (the
leaf is essentially mashed up with
the female mouthparts). Final cell
is closed off with a similar plug.
· Two flight periods: mid-April and
May to late July and again in August
to September.

CUCKOO BEES
...

· Cuckoo bees nest in whoever's gaff
they are trying to usurp. Overall,
cuckoo bees tend to have darker,
smokier wings. Often, cuckoo bees
are less furry, more sparsely haired
so that you can see the shiny black
body below. Though worn-out
workers can look similarly bare.
It's hard to tell a social bumble from
its cuckoo without a glass tube, a loupe
and a good guide (or someone who
knows what they are looking for):

*The Field Guide to the Bumblebees
of Great Britain and Ireland* by
Mike Edwards and Martin Jenner

Bumblebees by Oliver Prys-Jones
and Sarah A. Corbet

Guide to Bees of Britain by Buglife

THE MOST COMMON SPECIES ARE:
...

· Southern cuckoo bee
· Forest cuckoo bee
· Red-tailed cuckoo bee
· Barbut cuckoo bee
· Field cuckoo bee

ALYS'S THOUGHTS...

Getting Ready

For any beekeeper, winter is all about planning. Usually it involves intravenous levels of tea and cheap cake, and construction of frames, hives and equipment – all work to keep you warm. What I've come to realise, though, is that no season is ever quite like the last. You can make plans for expansion across these barren months, only to discover that you have severe losses in the spring and need to build up numbers again. Or you might build hundreds of honey boxes, ready for the bounty of honey, only for it to rain all summer. So, in brief, it's good to plan but always be ready to change and throw it out the window, because Mother Nature can chuck you some wicked luck sometimes.

From the texts I'm receiving, I'm guessing Alys has been using the time to swot up, the perfect thing to be doing on a winter's evening. I sense she might be starting to realise that beekeeping is a massive undertaking, but her worries are no different to anyone else's about this craft. I'm getting texts with questions like:

How much time and energy will the bees require?

Can I leave them for long periods?

What happens when they swarm?

I'm not going to be able to equip Alys with all of my knowledge instantly. This is graft you cannot master in a lifetime and I cannot possibly predict what is going to happen with her particular strain of bees across the season. But I can, at least, try to give her the basics.

Keeping bees has to be pleasurable. As a former travel and reportage photographer, I would often experience huge lulls between commissions. Waiting for the next remote assignment to arrive would leave me feeling a little insecure and anxious. I was clearly not naturally suited to being a freelancer or jobber, as it was known. I would counterbalance the anxiety by going fly-fishing in tiny gin-clear chalk streams in Wiltshire or by playing really quite appalling golf with fellow freelancers at Bromley Golf Centre. As well as lacking the correct golfing attire, I lacked consistency with work and would bumble from one job to the next, becoming very apprehensive about the next job to arrive via pager.

Today my bees provide me with a more consistent income and I'm less of a lounging drone. They give me uniformity and structure to deal with my days, which is similar to their own work ethic. I learned rather early on that failure to give them proper devotion and energy would result in diminished numbers and poor stocks through ill health and no crop for sale: it was that simple.

In the past, bees were kept in straw baskets called skeps and left to thrive on their own, and very little manipulation or assistance was required. A hands-off approach was appropriate. Beekeeping today is very different and mankind is partly to blame for the amount of intervention our bees actually require. Diseases and viruses that have been brought into this country by the importation of bee stocks require careful monitoring to prevent their escalation. The inconsistent weather has also become an issue and we are now forced to check our colonies more regularly for starvation.

Understanding the temperament of your bees is important. You have to get to know your bees and their unique qualities by regular handling. I believe this can only be done naked – well, with no gloves on anyway. Beekeeping for the hobbyist therefore has to be enjoyable. You can't have a hive of bees where you have to take a deep breath before entering in it. Or use overprotection with armoured chainmail and a bellowing smoke machine.

Across the various seasons, I've received my fair share of stings. On the face – lips, eyes, ears. On the septum is particularly painful. Stings on the stomach are bad but on the testicles is eye-wateringly painful stuff. How, I hear you cry, did I allow this to happen? All of these incidents have occurred because I had become negligent, careless and lazy with standard procedures. Not zipping my suit up correctly, leaving

gaps around my ankles for bees to crawl up inside my suits, getting out of vehicles and realising my veil has extra big holes in the face guard but carrying on regardless – all my own errors.

Plenty of beekeepers I have spoken with over the years believe the temperament of a bee strain is related to its production capabilities: strong, more aggressive bees are supposed to be more likely to give you a greater crop of honey than those more laidback bees which will let you tickle them with a feather.

I have experienced so many different strains of bees over the seasons and I have seen bees of both temperaments that have had bumper crops, but as a rule we use gentle bees in urban areas and more virile bees in the countryside. Any that don't perform or cannot be pacified will have their queen replaced at the earliest opportunity.

My wise chrysanthemum-loving grandfather Alfred used to say keeping bees was easy in your first year and that it would be in your second year that the learning curve would be rather sharp.

If you gathered a swarm from a hedgerow or a young nuclei, with a newly mated queen within your colony, it would be unlikely that they would be willing to abscond again that season and all would be relatively straightforward.

'I believe this can only be done naked – well, with no gloves on anyway'

STEVE'S THOUGHTS…

You would add on boxes as they became full and ensure the bees had enough stores of about 30-40 kilos for the winter.

Year two as a beginner would be a different challenge altogether and your beekeeping knowledge would have to be enhanced considerably. Bees would be wanting to swarm as soon as warm temperatures arrived. Swarming is a natural phenomenon, where the original queen leaves the hive with her flight force of workers to establish a new hive. This can happen for lots of reasons but lack of space could be one, the intensity of nectar flowing into the hive another. Or sometimes it is just because of the genetics of your bees – they have the instinct to want to swarm.

Either way, it can be rather alarming to witness a swarm of bees in the air for the first time. The reality is that the bees are relatively harmless during this upheaval. Yes, the sky can appear thunderous with the huge numbers of bees in the air at one time, but actually they are just searching for a new home and are relatively docile. Their bags are packed with honey for their journey and they are in search of a new gaff quickly before any weather changes occur. Various skilful manipulations would be required to keep them or you would just collect them when they swarmed and expand your numbers and not produce a crop of honey for their keeper.

The complexity of the colony's infrastructure is one that Alys will begin to fathom over her first season. They will not respond well to clumsy, unassured movements or being bumped or knocked from frames. There can be days when you can remove the cover board (a flat insulated board that sits on the top of frames and keeps the colony snug under the roof) from a hive and you can instantly tell, from the noise that radiates from inside, what the temperament and mood of those bees will be on that day. We have metal plates on the back of each hive, with notes about each queen inside and previous manipulations. However, that noise will give you a clear indication if all is harmonious or if open warfare is about to commence in your direction.

A warm summer's day with no breeze and with nectar flowing in by the kilo, or during the middle of the day, when most of the colony is away foraging, is the textbook time to be inspecting your bees. But in the summer months, we will often be amongst our bees when the sun is first rising or on a rooftop when it's setting, such is the amount of effort required to maintain our stocks.

If there is an almighty roar and immediate unrest from those first small forays inside, then all is not as it should be. A strong, instant growl could mean your colony is queenless and a new queen could be being created by the conversion of a larva, being fed royal jelly. Or perhaps she has died of old age or infertility or, as is often the case with inexperience, poor handling – perhaps she has fallen from the frames during inspections and is lost in the grass alone and under the inspectors' feet. If you smell overripe bananas, then you've got a problem as the attach pheromone of a honeybee is this rather charming, fruity odour.

Alys has chosen a top bar hive as a dwelling for her potential bee colony. It's a system I've very little practical experience with. I've only witnessed it in Africa – Zambia specifically – where NGOs often try and persuade local beekeepers that 'West is best' and bees need to be kept in these ground-dwelling hives. It is of course is a disaster there, as beekeepers have been effectively keeping bees using traditional methods for years, and the top bar hives sit around idly like coffins, whilst various bark and log hives swing from the tree tops and prosper, occupied by wild colonies.

Where bees have been domesticated and used on top bar hives, however, I've witnessed bees building freestyle on frames. Excess honey is cropped, usually from the extremities of the colonies, or cut from the edges of the brood.

Alys's choice of hive means she can't just leave her new colony in there to get on with things. I'm not talking about comb production, I mean she's going to have to be monitoring for levels of parasitic mite infestation underneath the combs from natural drop off and checking the colony is not starving during prolonged bad weather periods. This style of hive is also rather tricky to apply feed into as there is no space on the top bars, and so bags of feed or trays have to be placed on the edges of the brace comb they build. But if the colony is close to starvation then it can be too far away from a colony to find.

I can only advise so much on my visits as my own bees demand my complete devotion over the season and I have always found long-distance relationships tricky to maintain. Beekeeping is not something you can master over the Internet.

I don't doubt her devotion though. I know Alys has had chickens and manages her allotment almost daily, so I'm sure these bees will be cherished when they arrive. I know she will give them the attention they require. I'm still thinking about what strain or colony to donate.
I won't know until the weather warms and I can assess each for condition, strength and temperament – essential on an allotment with people pottering around.

It's going to be quite some adventure for Alys. I know the calls and texts are going to start coming when the weather warms and the colony's expansion is inevitable. I hope she is not going to become too frustrated with me when I'm not on hand to pick up the pieces.

STEVE'S THOUGHTS...

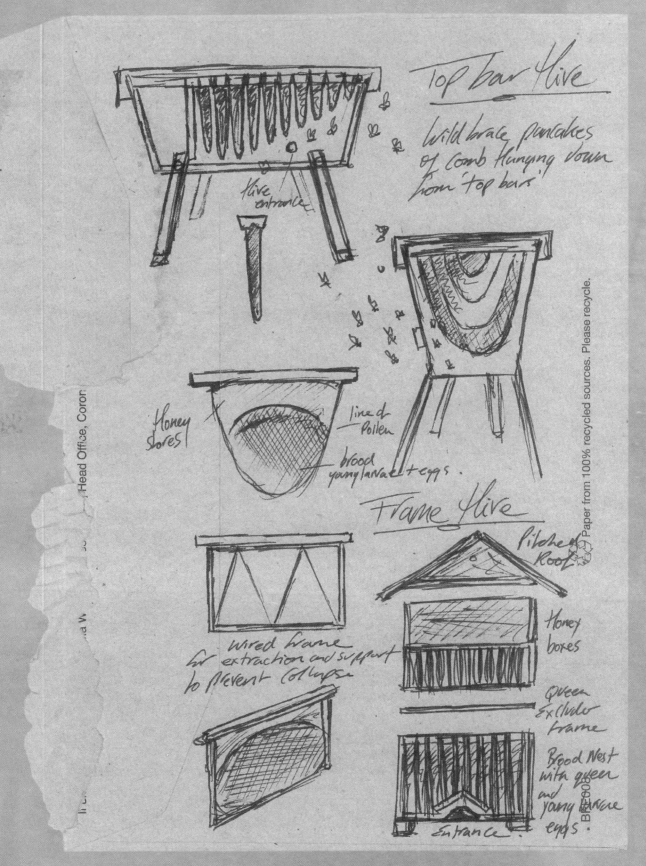

Top Bar Hive

Wild brace pancakes of comb hanging down from 'top bars'

Hive entrance

Honey stores

lined pollen

brood young larvae + eggs.

Frame Hive

wired frame for extraction and support to prevent collapse

Pitched Roof

Honey boxes

Queen Excluder frame

Brood Nest with queen and young larvae eggs.

Entrance.

Paper from 100% recycled sources. Please recycle.

Head Office, Coron

I love writing notes on the back of old envelopes – usually bills. This is a rough drawing of a top bar hive and its huge dinner plate pancakes that hang down, as well as a conventional frame hive below.

43

y

holy grail of protein and sugar, fat and carbs: buttered toast, cake, burgers, doughnuts, ice cream… You can't exist on one without the other – a life of all sugar or all protein is not only a chore, it'sunhealthy. Pollinators are just the same. Bees like nectar, but they need pollen justas much. Nectar is their carbohydrate of choice and pollen their protein. They require different amounts at different periods in their lives. Sugar is needed for nest building, for dashing between flowers and chasing after the opposite sex. For the actual act, you need a mixture: sugar to fuel desire and protein to create sperm and eggs and to raise the next generation.

Early plants relied on wind and waterto pollinate them. This is an extraordinarily risky strategy; pollen grains are as light and small as the tiniest specks of dust you can imagine. There's only one way that throwing your sexual parts to the wind works, and that's if you produce a huge amount. Wind-pollinated plants only get away with such odds because they produce so much pollen, as any hay fever sufferer can testify.

Insects offered something more. Pollinators don't sit still; they like to move around and that, to a plant stuck in the ground, is useful. Suddenly you don't have to be next door to your kin to have sex – you can move a bit further away, which allows you colonise new ground. Flowering plants co-opted pollinators so they could rule the world.

The earliest pollinators didn't exactly apply for the job, they sort of fell into it. Mostly they were beetles which sought refuge in early primitive flowers (these

would have looked a little like a magnolia). These flowers closed up at night and for the beetle that's a great bed – warm, dry and protected from predators. While they were getting comfy, some pollen got transferred onto them; the next night, settling into a different 'room', the pollen got knocked off and transferred to the stigma. The rest, as Darwin would say, is evolution.

Plants now started adapting themselves to lure the beetles in. And what the beetles liked most was pollen. It was rich in starch and protein, thus the more pollen you ate, the stronger you grew, and the better your species did. Beetles started seeking out flowers with more protein. What started off as anice bed for the night became a nice meal too, and the whole world began to shift as flowers started to evolve to please pollinators.

For pollinators, plants offer a feast of nectar and pollen. Nectar is a little like a soft drink: a mix of water, sugars, amino acids, lipids, proteins and sometimes other compounds such as antioxidants. Nectar is by far the most important reward from the flowering plant. Each plant has its own brew and the choice is as wide and varied as any soft drink aisle. Geta pollinator hooked on your brew and they will keep coming back for more.

The amount of sugar in the nectar varies greatly – anywhere from 7 per cent to 70 per cent – and can even vary between individual plants. There is a direct correlation between the concentration of sugar in a species and the pollinator's needs. Bees like a high concentration of sugar, somewhere in the 30-50 per cent range. Their tongues are specifically adapted to take up such sweet concentrations, whereas butterflies, who have long thin tongues that rely on sucking, rather than the bees' capillary action, require flowers with a much lower concentration – too viscose and the poor butterflies can't sup up the sugar.

Some nectar also includes alkaloids such as caffeine and nicotine, both of which bees in particular have a preference for. In fact, it turns out bees like drinking Coca-Cola – to them it tastes surprisingly like their favourite nectar flowers. It's been speculated that the caffeine in the nectar also helps improve the bees' memory, resulting in return visits to the flower.

Pollen is male sperm cells and insects get addicted to it much like body builders do to those protein shakes. It's estimated that a honeybee colony requires between 15–55kg of pollen every year. To put that in perspective, the top end of that is the equivalent of the weight of me in pollen! And if the point of pollen is to transfer sperm cells for the plant, the question is, why are plants allowing so many insects to dine out on their genes?

This is the pollination deal, if you like. It's known as mutualism. Pollen is much more expensive to produce than nectar and the plant has evolved to produce just the right amount of pollen, so that it offers the maximum amount of pollen transfer for the minimum reward.

Bees are well-adapted to collecting pollen; bumbles and honeys tend to collect it in pollen baskets, which are essentially a mass of pollen packed around specifically designed hairs that hold the grains together. Often you will see bees come out of flowers covered in pollen, and then you'll see them carefully clean this into the pollen basket with their forelegs. Of course, they can't reach all the pollen, or they might miss some, and this is how cross-pollination occurs.

With the garden in mind, it's tempting to want to provide some sort of definitive, catch-all list of the right plants for pollinators. Some would argue this would be all natives, others would shun any double petal forms or argue for all certain-coloured flowers, but the fact is pollinators are diverse. Some have specific needs, some don't, and none of them care much for rules – if it's got something they decide they want, they'll go for it. Thus, I have seen bumbles enjoy double roses and find something in a camellia so frilly that you can't imagine that there's any nectaries left.

However, there are a few guidelines that are worth sticking to when choosing flowers for pollinators:

· Stick to single flowers. Often when a flower has been bred to be a double

> 'It's estimated that a honeybee colony requires between 15–55kg of pollen every year'

The dots inside
a foxglove are
there to act as
a landing guide
for the bumblebee,
sending them
straight up to
the nectar source.

or possess a certain visual characteristic, it's sadly at the expense of pollen and nectar. Often double or semi-double flowers block the bees from accessing the pollen and nectar, or worse still there's no nectar at all, so although the plant may look alluring to both the bees and us, these flowers are all style and no substance.

· Plant as much as you can; fill every space (if nothing else, it will mean less weeding).

· A well dined-on garden is a bit like one of those great old American roadside diners – a comforting, filling pit stop that allows you to keep going on your journey, and with something to please everyone. In garden terms, this means lots of flowers, but also lots of layers. Different wildlife inhabits different spheres; some like to be high up, some like to shelter low down, some hang in the middle. An ideal garden has shrubs, trees and some climbers as well as flowers. Aesthetically, this works well too. A garden that has layers, that can't be seen all at once, has intrigue. Where does that path lead? What's behind that tree? It breaks up your view and even in very small spaces there's something far more enticing about a garden that is more than just ground

layer and boundary wall. It makes the most of your space, too.

· Although it's quite nice to think that come winter you can retire from the garden, insects need year-round food, so a garden that has something in flower every month is much more useful than a garden that is all bang and buck and over by July. Nectar in particular varies greatly over the seasons; in spring it is rich and sweet, but by autumn it has become dilute in some plants. The fluctuation peaks around midsummer, when there are so many species competing for pollinator services and any flower that is going to do well has to offer up a gourmet meal. By August the numbers of flowers are starting to decline, but there are more pollinators around, as the likes of the bumblebee colonies start to swell. At this point, it's a seller's market and even thin nectar does well.

'For many foraging insects, life is made easier if there's a mass of flowers to move across'

Our own native flora doesn't do a great deal come late summer, so this is when it makes sense to look further afield. There's a lot of controversy about the native versus non-native debate as far as food sources are concerned. Whilst everyone is still arguing, it makes sense, I think, to look at it this way.

ALYS'S THOUGHTS...

Near-natives, those that are in what's known as the paleoecological range (i.e. before we became separated from mainland Europe), are not a million miles away from what the insects' ancestors would have known. There's a chance that they adapted to eat off similar things, so if there are other species closely related to a UK native, there's a chance the bees are going to like these species too. An example would be, say, extending the range of geraniums, lavenders, lamiums, tansies and thymes.

We also know that bumblebees do well on perennial and biennial herbaceous plants. We know that they have a preference for three families when it comes to pollen. Bumblebees like the pea family (*Fabaceae*), mint family (*Lamiaceae*) and the figwort family (*Scrophulariacea*). The great tome on this is *Plants for Bees: A Guide to the Plants that Benefit the Bees of the British Isles*. Their top ten plants for bumbles include willow, rhododendron, vetches, thistles, brambles, birdsfoot trefoil, clovers, foxgloves and knapweeds.

The first lot are not necessarily the best plants for small gardens, let alone balconies. But foxgloves and knapweeds (*Centaurea species*) are uncomplicated to grow, pretty to look at and suited to a wide range of soils, and it's easy enough to get some clover into your lawn. You might not always be able to offer up a complete spread, but you can at least get one course in.

There are plenty of non-native plants that we know bees of all kinds love. Asters, such as *Aster frikartii*, New England aster or Michaelmas daisies (all found in the *Asteraceae* family) are good examples. Honeybees and bumbles are all made very happy by these late-summer flowers. Extending to other members in the family makes a lot of sense, so chrysanthemums, dahlias, rudbekias, gaillardia, thistles, goldenrods (*Solidago* species), everything from *Echinops* to globe artichokes and cardoons and hawkbits will suit honeybees, short- and long-tongued bumblebees and solitary bees.

For many foraging insects, life is made easier if there's a mass of flowers to move across – it saves energy if you can really feast in one sitting. In design terms this also looks better. As delightfully eccentric as those collectors' gardens are, having just one of everything tends to look fussy and rarely pulls a punch. Planting in odd numbers, threes, fives, and sevens mainly, looks far more pleasing and effortless than even numbers.

ALYS'S THOUGHTS...

21st February

Birmingham

Dear Ben,

I saw my first bumble of the season on Wednesday. So it starts, it means it's happening again. I always worry slightly that I have dreamt Spring up.

I'd received a surprise package of plants from a nursery and in it was a Hellebore 'Candy Love' in full flower, a lovely gift if ever there was one. It's flowers start off a delicate ivory and with age gradually deepen to a blush pink before fading to a dusky chocolate purple. The most graceful aging you can imagine.

It takes time to know where a plant should sit, you can't just go out and plonk it straight into the ground. I leave it in its pot and then try it out in various locations, till I find the one that suits it and me best. And whilst I was pondering the merits of a site,

there the buff-tailed bumble buzzed in.
That it chose to dine on a recent introduction
rather than the full buffet of other hellebores,
snowdrops, primroses and bean is I'd laid
out for it was, I guess, neither here nor there.
I pretended not to be hurt. 'Candy Love'
is as its name suggests clearly intoxicating.

It was heartening to see a bumble, to smell
the earth sweetening and see the dull winter
greens recede as the new growth stirs. Of
course its bitter again, the ground solid and
the wind whips through you. I am staying
inside and sowing seeds. February is
running away and the windowsills are
beginning to burgeon with seedlings. H
mutters darkly about this take over. I guess he
knows in a month or so he takes me to the
garden again and these seedlings represent
that march.
I hope the bitter winds didn't spoil Cornwall?
Did you brave the sea?

'It was heartening
to see a bumble,
to smell the earth
sweetening and
see the dull winter
greens recede as the
new growth stirs'

I'm in London editing next week so I
might try and drop by for a refill of
honey (can I bring my own jars?) Do
you want anything from the garden?
There's limited choice – winter salads with
chicories (tasting perfect, the frost has just
taken off their bitter edge), cabbage, potatoes or
Jerusalem artichokes (mountains of them, I
promise to put winter savory in this time).

Abby x

golden yellow collar

golden yellow band

buff tail but is only on the queen
all the workers have white tails with their faintest
buff line

3 February
A fleeting Devon trip

Josh and I make an early start and point the bee truck
in the direction of Devon for a pilgrimage to Buckfast
Abbey and the most divine Devon countryside.

It's going to be fleeting but I've spent weeks rereading
all my Brother Adam books and I know there have been quite
a few changes along the way to how bees are managed today
at the Abbey.

In brief, Brother Adam, an old monk is a legend in the
bee world for breeding a strain of bee called Buckfast.
He died in the early 90s after years of bringing various
strains of honeybees into the UK - usually in his pocket
- from around the world and probably spreading loads
of disease in the process. After his death, the bees are
run commercially for honey production - very unsuccessful,
massive investment, huge pressure. Something has to give.
Now, less about honey production, more about education and
a new person at the helm.

An artist who I've worked with on some children's workshops
has given me an introduction to Clare, the head of bees
at the Abbey.

Her office is in an old carpet warehouse and Josh and
I race down from London to get there mid-morning in time
for some tea and light chat about bees. I've got a Brother
Adam's book with me but I'm surprised to hear that history
is one thing the new era is not focused on.

Clare's bee knowledge is certainly extensive and at
first I'm a little unsure why this heritage is not being
preserved. I'm a little shocked to hear that not all
class Brother Adam in such esteem.

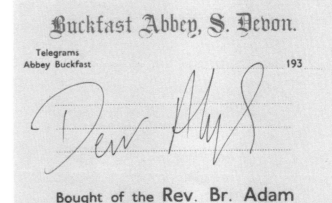

It seems little remains of his legacy at the Abbey – equipment has been sold or burned as disease was a problem, and what is refreshing is the emphasis on education.

I'm still thrilled to visit the mating and queen-rearing sheds in the grounds of the Abbey. The lichen-covered entrances are a picture; the salmon-painted sheds would not look out of place on the south coast. They are apparently that colour as the monastery had a huge batch of paint left over.

Across the years I have kept bees in a variety of different styles of hives. My first in London were the ornate, cottage-style hives, as that was what I had been used to in the countryside. As it happened, it was a real mistake as these hives are not very practical and have numerous components and were never right on a council block.

I have never attempted to keep bees on top bars, allowing them to build their own wild comb pancakes. There have been occasions though when I have miscalculated the strength of a colony and wild brace comb has been constructed in every available space – usually the roof cavity between the top box and the feeder. The result is always a mess as you break the weld and honey drips and oozes everywhere.

This can happen when a large flow of nectar is being brought in to the nest by the bees. The result is usually a disaster as combs become fused to any neighbouring surface and cross-braced to each other.

Clare in front
of a green mating
shed at Buckfast
Abbey, the only
real physical
remnants of Brother
Adam's legacy.

1: Brother Adam's
old queen-mating
shed entrance,
with weathered
alighting board.
2: Clare at
Buckfast Abbey,
monitoring for
Varroa mite drop
on a sticky board.

Therefore I decide to make a call to Phil Chandler,
the Naked Beekeeper - or the Barefoot Beekeeper, I should
say. Phil has been one of the main pioneers in top bar
beekeeping in the UK and has experimented with numerous
styles and formats.

Keeping bees for the sake of keeping bees has suddenly
become hugely popular and rightly so. Fifteen years ago
to keep bees outside of a conventional hive was considered
very hippy and not correct.

But bees have only been kept in hives for a little over
100 years, prior to that in straw baskets - anyway this
is different as this is about the bees themselves and
not exploitation for honey.

We meet in a bar in Totness and Josh is hooked and various
sketches and measurements are discussed. It appears to be
an evolving way to keep bees - no set rules or guides but
try something and see. It can't be good for London but
Josh likes the idea of its methodology for his olive grove
in Italy.

We are short on time and only have a few hours of daylight
left so we race up to a small coppice overlooking Totness
to view a few hives that Phil uses for teaching.

I see Phil also has some old original hives fused to the
ground from Buckfast Abbey. They were sold off - their
roofs still painted salmon-pink.

One hive has sadly died out - looks like starvation -
the others flying with pollen. Early brood rearing must
have started.

- S

1: A shrine to
Brother Adam at
the marvellous new
education centre
at Buckfast Abbey.
2: Weathered old
honey packaging
at Buckfast Abbey.

Alys and Phil
Chandler inspect
his bees in an
incredible top
bar hive near
Totnes, before
they turned nasty!

Planning

A GARDEN SHOULD HAVE:

...

A pond, however small, even if it's just a bucket with some stones for pollinators to rest on and a ladder for frogs to climb out with.

A tree or two that flowers and is followed by fruit that you and others might like.

A shrub or two that flowers and is followed by fruit. In a small space, plants have to work hard so blueberries, gooseberries and currants are all worthwhile; something for them, something for you.

Raspberries work well along fences, giving you and the bees much pleasure over the summer.

Some perennials that flower late into autumn: asters, chrysanthemums, Japanese anemones, sedums, rudbeckias and erigerons.

And **a scattering of annuals** that set seed where they wish: cornflowers, poppies, coriander, linseed and, best of all, marigolds that refuse to give up right into the frost.

Some biennials to look forwards to: foxgloves, forget-me-nots, verbascums, caraway and angelicas.

Some vegetables too, the lazy sort perhaps: globe artichokes, wild rocket plants for salads, mint for tea, herbs for cooking, elephant garlic that, if left alone for the first year, continues to produce forever. Or something truly seasonal: a courgette or two, a chilli in a pot that can be brought in for winter pickings,

a patch or pot of salads, a patch for potatoes. As long as your seed or plants are organically grown, all these will provide plenty of picking for you and the pollinators.

A seat somewhere sunny surrounded by flowers because sitting still is the best way to learn who visits your garden.

As many bulbs as you can squeeze in: around the base of every permanent plant, around your fruit bushes and raspberry canes, tucked into places that may be deep in shade by late summer. Sweeping along path edges, buried into pots.

A compost heap as large as you can afford, the more you make the better your garden and everything in it will grow. Spread it out every autumn and again in spring, marvel how it disappears below, nourishing all with good things to eat. A truly noble rot.

A dead hedge, a beetle bank, a pile of rotting logs, undisturbed secret places. Many insects need a place to hide during the day, particularly beetles. They need somewhere to rest over the winter. This place rarely needs to be visited; it's good if there's plenty of wood for things to burrow into, sheltered from the worst of the rain, that it is a little hidden from view.

A beetle bank is just that: a bank of earth covered with plants, rarely mown, somewhere to scurry home from after a night of hunting slugs. It makes the most sense near to where your vegetables are grown. Your beetle bank will appeal to many solitary bees, newts (if not too far from water) and small mammals.

ALYS'S THOUGHTS...

A dead hedge is a beautifully ramshackle thing. All those branches and tough bits that the compost doesn't want and neither does the bin collector. Gathered together, allow it to return to whence it came and whilst on that journey a new home for a thousand things is made. A dead hedge is only ugly if you fail to unearth the beauty in everything.

And if you have space, **a lawn to laze on**. A lawn should never be all green – how dull. Lawns should flower, daisies should run wild, dandelions should sing, speedwell should creep, violas should flourish in the shady spot, buttercups for the damp spots, stitchwort, ground ivy, early marsh and early purple orchids, woodruff, salad burnet, vetches, wild strawberries, herb Robert, bird's foot trefoil, black medic, century, kidney vetch, wild thyme, cranesbills. I've seen so-called lawns have them all.

The mower is dead; long live the flowers. OK, so maybe you like your mower. Here's the guide to a pollinator-friendly cut.

There are three types of long-cut lawn regimes. In all of them, it's very important that you remove the grass cuttings. This impoverishes the ground allowing more of the pretty things to move in. The lazy version: you mow if and when. This is great for lawns with lots of dandelions in them. You let them flower but before they go to seed, you mow. You should aim to leave at least a month between mowing

and keep your blade high, around ten centimetres because your grass will have lots of life in it.

A spring meadow: ideal for those who need a short lawn for the summer holidays, for cricket, football or just lazing on. It can happily accommodate aconites, snowdrops, dandelions, lady's smock, cowslips, knapweed, naturalised daffodils, such as our native Tenby daffodil, meadow saxifrages, field buttercups, early wild orchids, bluebells and if there's a little shade wind, anemone.

Make your first cut around the end of June, beginning of July and then cut until late autumn. Make sure your first cut is very high, around ten centimetres and slowly work your way down to a neater lawn. Always collect the clippings.

A summer meadow: This is the opposite, you mow from late September to early April (clearly you won't have to mow in December, January or February). This method is particularly good for summer butterflies and moths.

A summer meadow will have clovers, campions, cranesbills, cornflowers, sorrel, bedstraws, wild peas and vetches, hawkbits and hawkweeds, sainfoins and scabious. This doesn't have to be your whole lawn; it can be a patch, a rectangle under a tree, a swathe with a path mowed through. Even a patch will grow something interesting, but it may take time. If you want to increase the flowers, you can add wild plug plants of perennials.

'A lawn should never be all green – how dull'

ALYS'S THOUGHTS...

69

Planting

The compost for the Tate Britain garden arrives by giant truck on a warm spring morning. I managed to source it from Westminster City Council; it makes sense to keep it local. We're not talking a few bags here but six tonnes of the dark molasses gear. The driver is highly skilled at these manoeuvres and each bucketload is carried over the trees and onto the edge of the proposed site of floral devotion.

I'm not entirely sure, if I'm honest, what makes good compost, but I text a few pictures across to Alys, with the title 'good shit?' She promptly texts back to ask how it smells. The answer is 'honky', which apparently means it will have a large percentage of horse poop amongst it as it's from Hyde Park. That's good, right?

I decide the best thing to do is to put some into a jiffy bag and dispatch it up to Birmingham for an expert analysis. I'm hoping it's not going to cause a police incident and besides, I've been told I'm not sending enough letters.

Next, the plugs arrive. They look as if they are all dead – just twigs in soil. I text over a set of uncreative but informative pictures of what I think are dead plugs to Alys. I'm told to 'give them a chance' and 'give them some water'. I drag them out into the bee yard and borrow my neighbour's watering can, giving them a mighty drenching. By the end of the day they look a million times better – the twigs are alive for now.

The seed packets come next. I've not been honest here, and need to own up. I've ordered double what I was told to. I just want loads of flowers everywhere. I've also gone and sneaked in some of my beloved wood sage and some teasels. I've noticed a charm of finches around the Tate and they are going to adore these when they seed later in the year.

'So when do I sow these?' I ask Alys. Soon, apparently, so I buy cheap plastic trays with cloche covers from my local garden centre. These seeds are smaller than the ones we sourced from the tree in St James's Park. But I break them out and carefully plant them in the trays with a little grit and compost. I'm not expecting a rainforest by the end of the summer, but hey, from small acorns...

It's not a bad show of numbers for the first sowing day, considering the drizzle, although I think we have more spades and trowels than participants. A whirling dervish of red hair in an Aran knit is already hard at work with a hoe, marking out the boundary of the border, no discussion about design and planning – we are off.

Hoe marks show the area that's to be planted with a series of wavy lines, and the first thing I notice is that it's some distance from the yew hedge. Apparently nothing would be likely to grow next to it so there's no point planting or sowing up to it. Slowly staff members arrive, kindly donating time from their lunch breaks, some with trendy

Sowing the garden with the staff at Tate Britain. The ground was weeded, dug and raked before we started sowing.

London shoes and office clothing – and I was apprehensive about commitment!

Compost manoeuvring is the first task, as the six tonnes need distributing around the site, which has already been pre-hoed by Alys. This rich dark matter is wheel-barrowed by an ex-gardener and his colleague along with the rosy-cheeked Alys. I'm glanced at a few times and told to 'muck in'. I'm taking pictures, my first for almost a decade since I sold all my cameras, and it's stressful as I'm all fingers and thumbs and surely folk want a record for our book?

I try multi-tasking, which is useless, and I end up with compost on the camera, which now smells of fox piss when I put it to my eye to focus. Plant plugs are broken open from their plastic protection and dotted around the fringes; I notice that the cowslips are already placed on top of the compost by the large hollow log, a feature we've decided to leave.

Seeds follow; an old honey bucket is used to blend the mix. It is at this point that I own up, admitting I have not ordered five grams per variety but in fact ten grams of seeds per variety... what can I say, I like flowers. Apparently I've got a lot to learn.

My beloved wood sage makes it into the bucket to be mixed with sand, apparently easier to sow, but the teasels

are vetoed as they are not favoured by the gardener. I ask about more plugs and then I see a red mist – for me it needs to be a jungle of plants, like a temperate rainforest, with vines and stems blocking out the sun.

Apparently we have oversown anyway, as you are supposed to allow so many grams per square metre, so this should allow for a few leaving on people's feet I think. I also have noted the pigeons are enjoying what we have scattered.

There's been a good turnout of staff supporting the garden, plus a good number have passed and chatted to us. Even those at the windows overlooking the garden have been waving, I hope with approval.

A big bumble is also spotted at the end, its flightpath slightly hazardous above our heads. Alys and I both say it's a buff-tailed – a common variety to guess at!

March has been an excellent month for wildlife at the Tate site. At the start of the month blue tits were helping themselves to bees as they emerged from the hives – a sort of fast-food joint for birds. The blackbirds must have young already as they are constantly tossing compost around in search of grubs. I've also spotted seven coloured finches and a raptor... it's a sparrowhawk, a first for me in central London, which sends all

'I'm not expecting a rainforest by the end of the summer, but hey, from small acorns...'

I harvested some seed from my allotment so that a little of my garden could be found in London.

STEVE'S THOUGHTS...

1 & 2: We used young plug plants that we knew would be slow or difficult to germinate, or were biennials/perennials, where a jump-start would make all the difference.
3: Gently raking over the soil once you've sown the seeds helps to make sure they are settled, covered and less susceptible to becoming bird food.
4: Scattering yet more seed. It sometimes feels like you are throwing stuff to the wind, but if your ground is well prepared, nature will take care of the rest.

4

the small birds scattering as it swoops in through the crab apple trees which border the garden. It's in contrast to the stark surroundings of Tate Modern and the Penguin falcons which disperse pigeon feathers down from on high as they pluck their luncheon.

Oh, and I also spot a rat – but they are as common as pigeons in London, so nothing special there, except that this one is the size of a cat.

Josh, who works from our railway arch in Bermondsey, volunteers to build Alys's hive from salvaged items. Our own warehouse doors and fixtures have all been scavenged by Josh. Our shop counter is built from pallets and sofa castors and the mezzanine from scaffolding planks and poles – all constructed by Josh. His plan is to make the main carcass of the hive from an old Tate art crate. Bright yellow, these one-off units are used to transport artworks around the galleries.

We set him a budget of zero for this project.

The Royal Institute of British Architects sadly don't give out awards for beehives, but if they did, Josh's over-engineered beauty would certainly pick up a gong for best social housing made from recycled waste. Inside I've painted blackboard paint on the underside of the roof, for hive records, and scribbled a ditty – a note/letter of endearment for the gardener.

The top bars, from which the bees will hopefully build their wild combs, are old pallet struts and have a groove routed out of one side for a wax strip – a sort of guide saying please construct your home here.

The Perspex observation window is a skip find, the mesh Varroa floors are offcuts from my own hives, knitted together. Finally, the skip drainage pipe entrances are my favourite, and the discarded banner from a DIY store reads 'open' in large red graphic type. This is stretched across the roof board to keep the whole unit dry, and is visible when the hive roof is open.

It's a wonderful gift, constructed especially for the site. The bees would live in a shoebox but I think they will adore this artwork.

This palatial stately home has been forklifted onto the back of the bee truck and strapped down to prevent it from sliding around. It's going to require an army to move it into position – failing that, some retired allotment holders will do.

I spend close to an hour with Alys deciding on the spot, but the temperature is rising so I'm keen to get the bees installed. I'm encouraged by the giant limes that surround the allotment – they will be incredible for the bees in the coming months – but the hive needs to be far enough away so that it is not in their shade over winter, when the sun is not so high.

Sadly we have a fatality. The queen has failed in the skep colony, despite being carefully nurtured. This is so often the case in the spring; mature queens can run out of steam when they begin full egg laying. So I shake the flying bees in with the swarm. This is usually inadvisable and can cause fighting, but it's a new home and the bees are well mingled so any smells should be dispersed across them all.

Josh with the Tate's art crate, which formerly housed a Pissarro. Note his Health and Safety steel toe cap Aussie work boots!

STEVE'S THOUGHTS...

That spring, I waited for bees. It was a spring full of optimism, though waiting was somewhat tortuous as Steve kept changing the date. I felt so impatient to get going. I asked my friend Alistair, who has an allotment with his family on my site, to be my bee buddy. Al and I are very different people and I suspected his pragmatic approach would be much needed. I was right: my passionate, very emotional attachment to them wasn't always that helpful and besides, having company with the bees was an unexpected delight.

Steve and his friend Josh began to build my hive. It was the most beautiful thing, a brilliant yellow box of delights from an old packing case they sourced from Tate Britain that once transported a Pissarro. Once they came, I fell headlong for them.

The day we came to weed and sow our new garden, the staff appeared from all over the Tate. We had ground staff and directors, and a few came from Tate Modern. A few came for ten minutes and many more their whole lunch hour.

Our first winter had been spent busying ourselves for our new garden.

'It's hard to have that leap of faith in the beginning: oversowing seems such a simple solution'

We bought seeds suitable for shady spots from Pictorial Meadows, the company behind the Olympic Park wildflowers. Steve had pulled off the amazing feat of getting several tons of compost from the Royal Parks free so that we could enrich the soil for before sowing. We found wheelbarrows to borrow and ordered in a compost bin.

We made extraordinary progress, weeding, mulching with Steve's compost, which I feared had been sitting around for rather a long time at the parks, and scattering with weed seed. Steve panicked that we didn't have enough wildflower seed, that it wasn't distributed properly, that we should have ordered twice as much.

It's hard to have that leap of faith in the beginning: oversowing seems such a simple solution, but the system, the soil, only has so much energy and nature will make her choices whether you sow twice as much or not.

It's a steep learning curve, that one. We were both trying to get to grips with new subjects and learning to trust each other's opinions. We battled a little about that.

1: Seed I collected from my own garden to supplement what we brought in for Tate Britain. Seed collecting from easy-to-grow annuals such as *Calendula* and poppies makes a lot of sense; every autumn your garden provides you with enough seed to start many new wildflower patches. 2: Once the seed is scattered, it's important to rake it in. This makes sure the seed won't blow away or dry out on the surface of the soil, and it does keep the pigeons from eating the lot!

ALYS'S THOUGHTS...

'It was was the most
beautiful thing,
a brilliant yellow box
of delights from an
old packing case they
sourced from Tate
Britain that once
transported a Pissarro'

We covered the
garden at Tate
Britain with well-
rotted compost.
We used a thin
layer across the
whole garden. The
soil was thin and
hungry, so this was
partly to increase
the organic matter
and partly to give
the seeds a good
start in life.

Dumbo Feather Steve

Conversations with extraordinary people

10 pm - 2nd April

After 16 hours on trains,
eating crisps I have
learnt one very important
rule. When you come home,
Don't eat lettuce from
the garden in the dark.
Inevitably the first bite
will contain a slug.
Thank-you for the honey!
love A.

Steve Benson
London Honey
Company
Unit **6** Dockley
Industrial Estate
Rohol Road
Bermondsey
London SE16 3SF

www.dumbofeather.com

9 April

I receive a call from the Tate warehousing department
in Bermondsey to say that a selection of packing crates
have become available. I often see these crates on my
visits to the bees at the various Tate sites and I've
always wondered if one could be made into a hive.

A collection of Pissarros has been recently moved
(ironically one is called the Summer's Field) and
we all race round to see what we can scavenge.

I notice some of these yellow painted crates have already
been utilised by staff as giant planters in the yard
when we arrive. The strong gales though have left their
greenhouse without any panes and it looks somewhat sad
on the tarmac yard – like an art installation, maybe
a bit Tracey Emin.

– S

_____

From: alys@beemail.com
Subject: Letters
Date: 9 April

S,

There's a buff-tailed queen in the compost. She went in an
hour ago and hasn't come out. I spend £65 on a professional
bumblebee nest with infrared viewing. I carefully fluff
out the mouse bedding that is sent with it and, of course,
she chooses the hidden depths of a rotting pile of
rubbish instead.

Dear Alys

Thanks for a
great day rushing
around in Brum.
I also found your
gardening glove.

B

Bumbles often do this; the compost heap is, of course,
a perfect home. It's insulated, it's highly likely to have
had a mouse nest (or more likely a rat's), and they tend
to be situated in gardens, so there's a potential food
source. They are out of the way and mostly undisturbed.
I am as proud as Punch that she's taken up residency,
but it is rather an indictment of my compost skills.

A good compost heap should be regularly visited
and regularly turned. The more you turn compost,
the quicker it breaks down. The breakdown processes
happens via the masses; everyone is involved, slugs,
snails, rodents, bacteria, worms, fungi, nematodes,
millipedes, slow worms, frogs, protozoa and spiders.
You can build as many bug hotels, hedgehog hostels
and beetle banks as you like, but I bet that your
ramshackle compost heap houses way more wildlife.
It's a no-brainer: take waste, turn it into gold and
offer free bed and board to everyone along the way.

The trick to making compost fast is to get the recipe
right and turn it often. You need roughly equal parts
nitrogen to carbon – that's green to brown stuff.
The nitrogen is mostly broken down by bacteria.
This is a fast and furious process – it's like the fire
starter, if you like. You can feel this happening with
cut grass, it starts to burn up as the initial bacteria
move and start to break down. But as anyone who's left
a pile of grass to break down knows, it stops after
a while and turns into the odd pile of slime that just
sits there, because there's not enough carbon to fuel
the fire. Carbon acts like good well-seasoned timber:
it sustains the fire for far longer than any lighter can.
Get the balance right and there's enough to feed everyone.

The nitrogen is anything green – grass clippings, green
leaves, stems, kitchen peelings, stuff that rots fast.
The carbon is brown stuff – old stems, twiggy bits, dead

leaves, newspaper pages scrunched up, torn pizza boxes
and cardboard, those bank statements you don't want
to face. For every green layer, a thicker fatter brown
layer needs to follow: it's that simple. Nature does
the rest.

By turning the compost every now and then, you add the
necessary oxygen to the system to keep it going. The more
you turn, just like stoking the fire, the quicker the whole
thing breaks down.

Which is why my compost is a little bit of a poor
reflection on me. It's not been turned for months, and
consequently it surely houses mice, and I'd put good money
on rats living in it at some point. If you don't want
either of these in your compost then you need to turn it
regularly – both rodents are neophobic, unsure of
conditions that change regularly. Leave it alone and you
have a very fine rodent hotel.

A

12 April

We have germination!

I receive an email from Gemma at the Tate Estate to
say that she's spotted germination at the staff garden.
I load my bee overalls onto the back of the Vespa and
scooter over. When I arrive there are small shoots
everywhere and I quickly begin trying to take close-
up snapshots on my camera phone for Alys.

I ping them over straight away. A detailed picture
is required for identification, but I'm not sure
my phone is up to it. The first response is not good.

She thinks they are weeds that have been brought
in by the compost I've sourced – amateur.

The second picture is more promising; she thinks it
could be a wood sage seedling. They are in tight clumps
and I haven't got a clue at this stage what I'm looking
at. I'm quite pleased with the nettles – some varieties
flower, I think? The cowslips are also flowering and
look incredible against the aging tree trunk.

– S

From: alys@beemail.com
Subject: Letters
Date: 18 April

Dear Steve,

You never read any of this, do you? I send you letters,
I send you files, attachments, Dropbox invitations, and
you never open any of them. Why do I keep writing then?

The bees will appear two weeks from now. I am terrified.
Terrified that I have signed up for too great a commitment
using the top bar system. I watch endless YouTube videos,
trying to get to grips with hive management. I have
no idea why you agreed to this system. Surely you can
see it's madness for a beginner?

The only thing to draw from this is that I really
am that bossy.

A

19th April

Ben

I wanted to tell you this, but
somewhere in that sunlit by sad
conversation about fruited avenues and
lost greens, I felt too shy to say it.

Last week at the university, whilst
teaching outside I came across a bee
on the floor. The hives had been buzzing
all morning and I knew that if I left
her there she would most likely get
squashed as she sat on the path to the potting
shed.

So I picked her up and looked around
for something to please her. All I could
think of was to offer up some water.
So dipped one muddy hand into the
watering can and made a small well of

water in my palm. A distinctly
earthy drink, but something never the
less and then I carefully transferred
her from one palm to the other.

She drank and very meticulously washed
her face and antennae.

I stared so hard and so close so that
I could see every detail. And only when
I was an eye ball away from her did it
occur to me that she was staring back
just as hard. And there we stood
looking at each other's strangeness.

And then, I felt her murmur, her
whole body vibrate and for a second
my heart missed a beat, had I made
her angry? And like that she was
gone, high up into the sky.

That moment when you feel the
engine start up, like an old mower

'Those precious
seconds before
flight – that
is what I wanted
to tell you about'

humming and buzzing into action, is really quite something.

Those precious seconds before flight - that is what I wanted to really tell you about. That I felt the moment and I felt as alive as she did.

Lots of love B.

18 April

The warm weather means the colonies are advancing
at a tremendous rate and the nests are booming –
I fear there will be a lot of swarming way before
the merry month of May.

I'm also getting texts from an anxious and expectant
mother: 'When are my bees arriving?'

Long-distance relationships in the past have not really
worked for me. I once dated someone in Hong Kong for
two years, long before the internet, and we met up only
twice in that time. Even with the bees on distant sites,
I don't just abandon them. I rely on someone local to tell
me what's happening with the weather and if the bees are
out flying.

So it is with trepidation that I am now about to enter
into one with Alys and her bees, and I know that I'm never
going to be around when she really needs guidance. I do
have bees in Shropshire and pass Birmingham at odd hours
in the day, but nighttime beekeeping is inadvisable.
You always get stung.

– S

1 May

Deeply disappointed. No bees. The beekeeper is too busy
to deliver them on Friday. He has a five o'clock meeting
he has to attend in London so there's no time to swing
by here first.

I have to wait another two weeks.

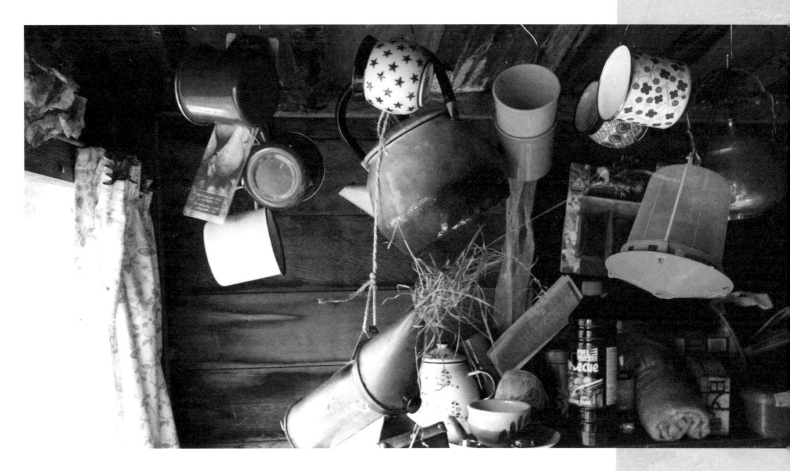

Steve's donated smoker hanging proudly in Alys's allotment shed.

All the bulbs I planted for their arrival will be over by then.

I was telling my mother all of this, bemoaning that strangely crushing disappointment of waiting patiently for someone or something only to have hope dashed at the last minute. It's such an ordinary sort of sadness, that of expectations not met. And as I was moaning on about this, looking out into the garden from the kitchen, the purple of all that honesty and the lilacs coming out glowing in the dark evening gloom, a sparrowhawk swooped

1

in after a great tit. A fighter pilot in suburbia dodging fence panels. I've never seen a sparrowhawk here before. So furious and fast and then that strange silence when all the small birds go into hiding. I wonder if it will return?

– A

12 May

Alys's bees are here...

I make an early start to avoid the traffic and the heat of the day and wrap the base of the skep with an old curtain. The straw of the skep will allow air in through the gaps for cooling the bees.

It's the first time our dogs have met, and Teal, my newly adopted Shropshire Lad, pees straight away on Alys's kitchen floor... morning!

Her kitchen is awash with seed trays on all available surfaces, and condensation is streaming down the windows – this is a temperate rainforest of germination on a large scale. I'm made tea in a commemorative royal mug and then follow the dogs out into the garden.

Her garden is incredible, and full of insects. It's divine, and I soon realise that there is nothing here that's for show. Everything seems to have been grown for a reason; it's either being cultivated for the table or being grown for pollinators. It doesn't take long to spot my first bee, a bumble – and it's off to what appears to be one of the hundreds of purple alliums – see, I know some flowers!

2

1: Tea, always essential before any work can start.
2: Me with the hounds – and the bees in the back – on the way to the allotment.

1

1: Inspecting the
hive from below.
A mesh floor allows
debris and the
dreaded Varroa
mite to drop
through, but
it also means
you can see the
bees. It smells
lovely underneath.
2: As the hive
is made from
recycled wood,
there were a few
holes from its
previous life of
holding a painting.
The bees decided
these would make
excellent exits.
Steve taught me to
plug gaps with
grass, a free,
sustainable
hole-filler.

It's a calming space after a drive from London, but there
are bees in the back of the truck and a hive to unload.
The bees quickly cluster onto the bars on the roof as
we scrutinise their world through the observation panel
at the rear. It a voyeuristic moment that we both become
aware of and so close up the side and let them settle in.

I'm fully aware that the questions about their care
will soon be arriving; it's only natural when you take
on this level of responsibility, and I'm delighted that
Alys is committed to this project. My only hope is that
I have time to deal with the flood when it arrives -
and it will arrive.

- S

22 May

I went to peek through the window at the bees, who
have now become architects of their own lives. The comb
that fell on the eco floor is slowly being fused to the
other combs, each with their own branches making them
impossible to lift. It's quite marvellous and beautiful,
but it doesn't make for easy beekeeping.

Steve promised he will come up next week and help rectify
things. I have to hope that the queen is laying. I picked
mint and put it around the base of the hive to deter ants.

I can't help but love the wild bees a little bit more with
every viewing of the honeys. I do nothing other than what
I do best, provide forage, and they do what they do best,
going about their ways, and we both are happy. What is this
obsession with honey anyway?

- A

**Steve added
a viewing window
to the hive and
it has been
invaluable.
You can wonder
at the bees and
their marvellous
work with very
little disturbance
to them.**

1

1: My first few combs were all sorts of strange shapes, but it was thrilling to see the bees busy with life. This was my first relatively straight comb, and you can see how pleased I was with it, even though it was the bees – not me – that did the hard work.
2: My bees and I get acquainted.

1: Alys's bees
arrive – a swarm
from a tree at
Tate Modern. They
were to go on to
produce colossal
amounts of brood,
despite continuous
harassment.
2: Alys's incredible
top bar hive
made from an old
Pissarro artwork
travelling case,
with a note from
the beekeeper.
3: The perfect
comb, well almost,
being removed by
the now confident
beekeeper.

1

2

1: Alys's hive
settled on her
allotment in
Birmingham in warm,
spring sunshine.
2: Wild, unwanted,
wonky braced comb
being removed with
gardening gloves
and tweed – it's
a look!

One of the great
joys of owning
bees is being able
to sit by the side
of the hive (never
sit or stand in
front of the flight
path) and watch
them come and go.
You learn a lot
about their
foraging habits
from this, and
it's a wonderfully
meditative position.
It sounds
lovely too.

BEE BEE TREE

...

I first became aware of the great beemaster Geoff Hopkinson through his regular columns in the national beekeeping magazine *Beecraft: The Informed Voice of British Beekeeping.*

Now in his early nineties, Geoff was awarded the British Empire Medal back in 2012 for services to beekeeping, which is a worthy achievement alone, but I became fascinated by his devotion to one particular tree, *Tetradium daniellii* or the Chinese bee bee tree, which he would regularly champion.

In the 1960s he even managed to secure some seeds from the Morris Arboretum in America. He also discovered a tree by chance, one late summer in St James's park at the back of the Churchill War Rooms, having noticed pigeons pecking at the seeds around the tree's base.

Not only did Geoff manage to germinate these prolific growing seedlings, he also managed to secure their planting in military fashion in a variety of locations around the UK.

What's intriguing about the bee bee tree, though, is the prolific nectar and pollen it can yield late into the season, when most plants and trees have peaked.

I inadvertently discovered this on the roof of Fortnum and Mason one autumn: I witnessed my bees returning late in the season with their pollen baskets laden and their tummies full when all should be barren.

So, it was on one late grey October morning that I decided to invite Alys to St James's Park to help me hunt down this incredible tree and hopefully find some of its precious seeds.

If you had witnessed us on that particular day, you would have seen a red-headed woman flailing around on the shoulders of a season-weary man, whilst plucking a slight tree of its glorious offerings.

The seeds had not fallen and were stuck inside their husky casings, but they were ripe and ready to fall.

We only manged to procure a small handful as my crumpled limps were no tower.

I received none of this valuable harvest; we thought they stood more of a chance with a professional germinator, rather than with someone who would be likely to forget them and who had other areas of devotion.

Of course, germination was achieved and the trees grew quickly. I'm hoping to one day see my children and take custody!

'Of course, germination was achieved and the trees grew quickly'

STEVE'S THOUGHTS...

Bee bee seeds straight from the tree and folded into a paper wrap for storage. Once I had cleaned up the seed, I tested them for viability by placing the seed between damp sheets of kitchen paper, putting them into a clear freezer bag and keeping them somewhere warm. This is a very quick method to get the seeds to germinate. If you put ten seeds between paper, and five out of ten germinate, then you know you have roughly 50 per cent germination. This can determine how many you have to sow in order to get healthy seedlings.

Feeding

A beautiful plant is a happy one. A field of dandelions can be as breathtaking as a rare poppy or a cultivated rose in bloom. What catches your breath is that these plants look beautiful because they thrive.

There are many tricks to how you make your garden look beautiful. You can cheat and pump your plants with manufactured fertilisers. Though the aphids can spot that trick a mile off and move in quick. You can endlessly replace your plants with new ones from a garden centre, so nothing looks too aged, overgrown or faded. Though the environment, the peat bogs, your watering bill, your fuel bill and your pocket all feel that cheat. You can play God and water more or less, offer up tonics and balms, pots and potions. There are rows of bottles offering small chemical miracles in every garden centre for this reason. But the happiest of gardeners, the sort that have a certain ease and grace that comes with few problems, all employ the same trick. They understand their soil and marry this with the right plants. And they make great compost.

Compost is everything: it's the beginning and end of life; it solves most, if not all, of your garden problems. Your soil is too heavy? It breaks it up. Your soil is too thin, too hungry? It bulks it out and offers up food. It locks in water, suppresses weeds (when made well; when made badly it does the opposite), it keeps soils warm in winter and cool in summer, it prevents erosion and compaction.

All you have to do is take your waste from your kitchen and your garden and pile it up somewhere not quite in view, but not quite out of sight either, in a somewhat orderly manner and wait a bit. Then every autumn, when growth has died back and every spring when growth is just getting going, you spread it out. The rule is spread mulch out in autumn on clay soils and in spring on sandy soils.

A thick layer, a couple of inches deep, around every bare bit of ground you can see. Don't pile compost right up around the base of trees or shrubs, they don't like it, everything else doesn't care much.

HOW TO MAKE GOOD COMPOST
...

Compost is best made somewhere contained. A bin, a box, a heap, it breaks down quickest if there is mass that can keep warm. It only breaks down quickly if there is the right ratio between carbon and nitrogen. You need 25-30 parts carbon to one part nitrogen. To make this simple: carbon is seen as brown stuff and nitrogen as greens. You need roughly equal parts of 'greens' and 'browns' by volume.

Greens include grass clippings, fresh weeds, fresh soft plant growth such as prunings, vegetable peels, tea bags, coffee grounds, animal manures from vegetarian animals (everything from cows to hamsters) and their bedding. If the animal is a lion then you need to rot their manures down separately before adding it to your compost. This prevents pathogens entering your soils.

ALYS'S THOUGHTS...

Browns include cardboard, waste paper, shredded bills, newspaper, toilet roll tubes, tough hedge clippings, woody prunings (the smaller you chop them up the faster they disappear), old bedding plants, old compost, sawdust, bracken, wood shavings, fallen leaves, manuscripts, paper bags, dried plant stems, pizza boxes.

Things that are neither brown nor green, but also add to the mix, include eggs shells (must be crushed first), hair, nail clippings, old jeans, wool socks, cotton underwear (no one else wants it), floor sweepings (as long as it's all natural), cotton tea towels, leather gloves, pet hair.

Unless you have a specialist composting system like a bokashi bin, hot box or green cone biodigester (all designed to take food waste) you should never put in cooked food, meat, fish, dog or cat faeces, disposable nappies, coal or coke ash. All of these carry the potential to either pollute your compost or harbour pathogens that might cause disease. Mostly though they attract rats. And nobody wants rats.

Compost is easily made as long as you remember to layer up, a layer of brown, green and so on. It's quickest if the layers are not too deep. It matters that the compost is neither too wet nor too dry.

'Compost is everything: it's the beginning and end of life; it solves most, if not all, of your garden problems'

If it smells it is usually because it is too wet and the conditions are becoming anaerobic; add more browns to sup things up. If it's too dry, water it and add more greens.

If you have lots of perennial weeds like bindweed, couch grass, docks, brambles and dandelions, stuff that most humble compost systems won't kill (you need very high temperatures to do that), then rot the weeds down in a bucket first. This is known as weed soup. When your compost is too dry, water it with the biologically active and nutritiously smelly weed soup – that way nothing is lost from the system.

Your compost is ready when it is dark brown, crumbles, holds its shape when scrunched together, but instantly breaks down again, it smells sweet and you can't see any of the constituent parts, though if you look closely you'll see it's teaming with life.

You should see your compost like a savings account. It is your future riches; it means healthy soil, lots of worms, and happy plants and bees. Never let anything out of your system; if you can rot it down, put it on the pile. You want to keep all that gold for your garden.

ALYS'S THOUGHTS...

119

THE TOWER OF LONDON

L 130

A TUCK CARD

Dear Beekeeper

Perhaps we should plant here everywhere?

Fill seed tray with good quality PEAT-FREE seed compost.

Carefully place seed ontop on compost and lightly press in (do not bury them in more compost). Cover the seed with a thin layer off grit or sand. Light seems to play a part in germination so do not bury them too deep.

take out of water

Sit tray in water until the top is damp and place in a clear plastic bag. Put in fridge for 1 week. Remove to sunny windowsill @ 21°C Keep clear plastic bag on until you see seeds appear. CROSS FINGERS.

Flowering

A busy summer. A film company asks if I'm keen to provide beekeeping services for a new film. It's about an ageing Sherlock Holmes, played by Sir Ian McKellen – I have to say yes, right? I agree to numerous days filming, which I later regret as I feel I'm cheating on my bees and not offering the level of devotion required. It also means I've not been on hand with advice as often as I would like for Alys.

But I manage a second trip to Birmingham in late August. There's a tiny chunk of honeycomb in a parfait jar on the work surface. The wax is dark, a sign that perhaps larvae have pupated in it prior to being filled with honey.

Of course I can't resist a taste. It's got a lime flavour but there is something even stronger – I can't quite put my finger on it. Alys is thrilled with the honey, the only amount harvested to date from her hive – I'm really surprised as the rest of the country has been reporting bumper crops but I know this is less about the honey for her.

Outside, the garden is turning and the fruit trees at the end of the garden have the most incredible bright red apples. I'm tossed one but told they have moth damage so look out for grubs. The flavour is so sweet and intense. The juice is refreshing and I scoff down the lot, forgetting about aforementioned grubs.

Dogs are loaded into the truck and we drive the short distance, as I believe I'm returning with some plants for the Tate garden. Alys's beekeeping style is along the lines of – well, if Miss Marple did beekeeping, then that's the look. Think tweed jacket and gardening gloves. I like it.

We open the twelve-foot high, razor-wire fenced gate and see the bees are flying in the late summer sun and appear truly settled. It's always nerve-wracking opening a hive whilst being watched. I used to be clumsy with anxiety when my mentor David watched me. A huge cloud of bees would engulf me at first, but not him, and my movements were not gentle and precise. I had plenty to learn all those years ago.

Now Alys seems confident but more smoke is required. The smoker I donated is lit but left on the ground. Bees bubble too much and you should only be seeing heads as you look down the frames. It seems it's there as a comfort blanket, lit at the beginning, puffed briefly, then ignored.

Stores are low, and I wonder if this is because the bees have not been really given the chance to forage but have spent the summer building then rebuilding their home – under the planning officer's guidance! They will need feeding soon if they are not allowed to procure their own stores. Made from beet or cane sugar is fine, it's raw or brown sugars that can contain impurities that are problematic.

Each frame is heavy, but not from stores – it's incredible how much a frame of sealed brood can weigh and can be

deceptive when you heft colonies in the autumn for stores.

I spot the hair clips used to hold comb in place, which are almost encapsulated in wax but appear to have done their job. An ingenious solution – I never would have thought of that.

Whereas Alys has devoted her days to tending her bees and comb uniformity,

I've avoided the garden, adamant that it will look after itself. At first I had been told not to water. But now after a long, dry summer things are looking a little floppy and I fear I have killed the damn thing. There have been complaints also from those who, like me, were expecting instant floral splendour. I'm to blame, I just have not been able to find the time.

STEVE'S THOUGHTS...

That summer with those bees felt like climbing a mountain at times. Top bar beekeeping, it turned out, had so very few proponents, so very few rules that weekly you had to make up your own. Steve was often baffled by my telephone descriptions of what was going on. I bumbled through those early days. I was not used to failure and I felt very emotional. Everything was an endless open-ended question. I wanted simple answers and there weren't any. The bees, being brilliant architects of their own worlds, refused to stick to my bars, refused to read the books I had, refused to see sense. I bashed through their world like a clumsy bear and they stung me to remind me of such. Still, very slowly, I started to see patterns, to not panic and see the process. Al and I endlessly Googled and YouTubed until we had answers. I sometimes felt furious with Steve for giving me this gift that required so much attention. In return, I had given him a garden that required so very little and even then, he didn't always give it that.

It was a long, dry spring and that made germination a little erratic. I kept pressing him to water the garden, to buy a sprinkler and just turn it on once in a while. To pull a weed out every time he went past – just one weed, I implored! But he was busy chasing bees and I was busy chasing the answers to mine. We battled. We fought. I felt like he didn't have faith in me, my garden or my strangely hippy method of beekeeping. I tested him terribly. He tested me back. Yet, despite this, neither one of us gave up. Neither did my bees. Neither did the wildflowers in our garden.

I went to wild camp on Dungeness on my own and visited his bees. He hid me a present of tea, a camping stove, a little milk and something for breakfast in an empty hive. I melted. I would master the bees, I would shepherd their wax into straight frames, and I would weed Tate Britain, alone if necessary.

I was stubborn. I persisted with my strange methods, often to Steve's amusement. Tate Britain turned to a sea of nettles at one point and I thought, 'Ah ha, that's why they were giving the compost away,' as I pulled out more nettles with bare hands. A six-hour round trip to pull out weeds when you forgot gardening gloves or hand tools felt like I was being punished for falling for Steve's world.

> 'I bumbled through those early days. I was not used to failure and I felt very emotional'

ALYS'S THOUGHTS...

4 June

Wet, wet day. I looked briefly at the hive yesterday and
could see that they are starting another two combs. I can
also see more cross combing. I know I need to get in there
and sort this out, because every top bar hive website/blog/
YouTube video/forum says be bold, rectify early. However,
this system is so far away from Steve's experience, and
like all novices, my questions are so vague, and we
(actually he) just end up frustrated with the whole thing.

I was left slightly wobbly on the phone, saying, 'Oh no,
it's fine, I'll be OK on my own, I'll just muddle through
somehow.' But it's not fine. I'm totally confused as to
what I am supposed to do next. I can't let them keep cross
combing because they'll either be a mess or, from what I
can understand, have a terrible time this winter when they
can't move efficiently to their stores.

Oh God, what have I done?

- A

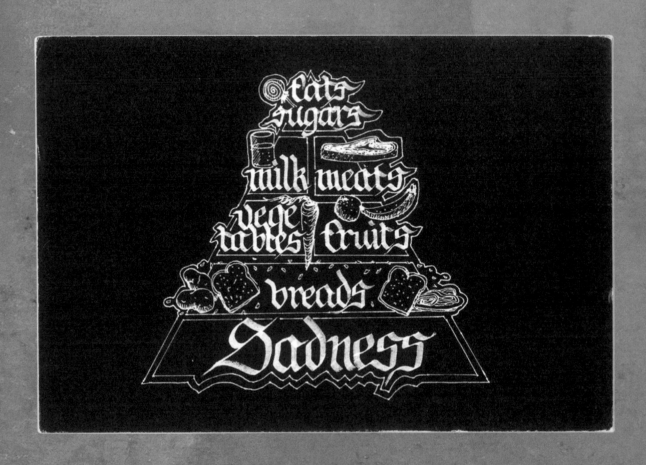

Sarah Tillman
"One could survive on the taste of sadness for years …"
2005
Illustration from Salvador Plascencia's novel *The People of Paper*

I will say too much about
beekeeping to you. It's
lonely, sad, demoralising
crushing, but mostly
heart-breaking.
I think I've found the one
thing I can't survive.
Most through I just
feel I look.
Love me and none.

Steve Benbow
The London Honey
     Company
Unit 6
Dockley Estate
Rouel Road.
Bermondsey
London SE16 3SF

28 June

We have flowers at the garden. There have been a few small
numbers popping up but nothing substantial to speak of.
There have also been a few problematic flowers; I've been
texting images of them to Alys. There's deadly nightshade,
which I think looks pretty but apparently is, well, deadly.
There are also collections of flowering weeds, which the
insects seem to love, so are staying for now.

The main flowers on this visit are the poppies, which have
sprung up above the nettles - I can recognise these - and
there are many different colours, and yes, the good news
is there are bees in them... Bingo.

- S

3 July

Where has the month gone? We now have twelve frames with
various sizes of combs. We have tried to right two very
wonky combs using two hairclips and some electrical ties.
One worked well, the other, heavy with honey, dropped and
is now being braced to the floor.

We've had a huge population explosion. The amount of bees
is dizzying and would be terrifying if they weren't so very
gentle. We've long given up smoking them before going in,
and often go in without gloves.

They seem happiest if just allowed to carry on working -
smoking them just panics them into consuming honey in a
fit of fear. I'm no bee, but when terrified, when someone
drives too close to the bike or takes a swipe at my life, I
quickly fall into fight mode. I can understand that a bee
with its stomach full of honey may be slower, but it makes

sense to me that it's also angrier. Perhaps that's naïve – truth is, I can never keep the smoker alight.

The downfall of the top bar hive as far as I can see is that our current frames, which are 38mm wide to allow for drone hatching, just seem too big. Often we get two combs per frame, which then knocks the next frame out as they inevitably brace across to strengthen it. For a top bar hive to work, you must have straight comb, and the bees naturally start straight at the middle but curve the ends outwards. It makes sense as this makes a structurally stronger set-up, but it means endlessly cutting and pushing back the edges to persuade them to keep on the straight and narrow. I can see why the Rose hive works better by allowing a gentle curve.

I am also aware that my wax shepherding is not that good. It's a constant battle between manipulating the comb and leaving the bees alone long enough to rectify the damage. I long for those strong, sturdy straight combs you see on YouTube.

Still, despite all of this, Al and I are getting better at the job – we are more confident at making decisions and we can now accurately spot both eggs and various sizes of brood, which means fewer accidents when we try to shepherd the wax into place.

One of the greatest and unexpected pleasures of keeping bees is Al. I love his humour, his unflappable nature. I often find him just sitting with the bees, watching them – he's one of life's great observers, quick to notice change. I look forward to his company as much as the bees on our weekly visits. I can see that many find the solitary aspect of beekeeping pleasing, but for me, it's this growing friendship that makes it so much fun.

– A

Attributed to Auguste Belloc: Nude, 1850-52
Akt · Nu
Chalon-sur-Saône, Musée Niepce

A little erotic floral photography
never goes a miss in a man's life
I'm off to Italy, I will return
in a while. Meet at
Tate Britain, any Thursday
or Friday to do some
weeding. Am happy
to go alone if you are
too busy, but as always
your company makes
it far more enjoyable
♥ A

London Honey
Company
Steve Benbow
Unit 6, Dockley Rd
Industrial Estate
Estate Dockley Rd
Bermondsey
London
SE16 3SF

Also reproduced in *Early Erotic Photography*, Benedikt Taschen Verlag

133

3 July

I first meet Sir Ian eight stories up at Fortnum and
Mason's beehives, my chosen venue for his introductory
lesson. I've got a month to get him looking like a bee
master as he's playing a 93-year-old Sherlock Holmes,
so his bee knowledge would have been extensive and
manipulation with bees confident and assured.

He's excited like a small boy and hungry for knowledge
when we meet. I start with a small honey tasting with
a few sticky jars I have in my rucksack - light and
delicate Hampshire Borage, complex Yellow Melilot from
Salisbury Plain, then the taste-bud-exploding London
Honey. He's hooked on the lot.

Then it's on to the bees...

It takes a while to don a bee suit over a kaftan, but
I know now it's achievable and still looks stylish when
I'm done.

Ian (I'm told to drop the Sir address straight away)
is hesitant but curious as I remove the vaulted oak
roof of the ornate hive with the Roman facade and lean
it against its solid-oak front leg.

I'm about to start when Ian asks to see my hands.
I've already explained I want him handling bees without
gloves by the end of our time together, but I can see he
has a plan. 'Hand double,' he pronounces. 'Not a chance!'
I shout back - he laughs loudly.

It's a really warm day so the bees are calm, plus
I've chosen some lambs to demonstrate with first;
no point starting open warfare with Welsh Blacks,
the Exocet missiles of the honeybee world.

By the end of an hour-long lesson he's handling frames
and chatting — always chatting, asking questions... he's
a fantastic pupil. We arrange to meet again in two weeks
and I warn him: it will be no gloves and less chainmail.
He laughs as we leave the cold of the building and then
he's gone in the bright light of the street, all beads
and kaftan and spotty socks, with a frame to practice
frame removal and rotation.

— S

7 July

I'm blaming everything on the bees from here on in. They
stole my heart and swarmed into my thoughts. Every time I
go to pull a weed or deadhead a flower, I literally hear
a murmuring. My honeybees not only like their spot at the
bottom of the allotments, but they seem a little obsessed
with my actual plot. So many mobbed a parsnip flower that
it fell over with the weight of them. And when the bumbles
decided to rob every fava bean flower, the honeys came
to my rescue and dutifully ignored the nectar and collected
great packages of pale grey pollen, thus I am now knee deep
in shelling. This winter will be a feast of dried beans.

Not that I favour my honeybees over the wild bumbles
and solitary bees, I know who truly does the work behind
my tomatoes and apples. But when your world shifts to the
vision of an insect, it's suddenly hard to be a gardener.
Every instinctive gesture to tidy up and whisk away
is the wrong one. Hence now not only do I have towering
parsnips ready to set seed, but a host of radicchio coming
into flower too. It looks quite something, the flower heads
are all easily twelve feet high, the fading acid yellow
of the parsnip next to sky-blue radicchio flowers.

— A

9 July

The new compost bins have arrived and are positioned
behind the yew hedge. They consist of three substantial
bays. I help for a few hours with the deforestation
of nettles but can't seem to fathom why Alys is using
her bare hands – blimey she's tough this one.

- S

9 July

My hands are raw with nettle stings from Tate Britain.
I spent all night dipping them into vinegar, rubbing on
various creams and wrapping them in cold flannels hoping
the madness brought on by itching would pass. Today they
are pinpricked red and every movement feels like tiny glass
shards are breaking under the skin.

I got to Tate Britain to find I'd only packed one frankly
useless glove. Two hours later and I was a mass of white
welts. Thank goodness for lovely Laura, Karen and Julie
turning up after a frantic Twitter call-out for a rescue.
Their good company, sound advice and humour saved me and
the garden.

Five builders' bags of weeds later and the garden can
breathe again. One end, nearest the Thames, will I think
look truly pretty next year. There's sweet rocket, honesty,
foxgloves, *Ammi majus* mallows and the odd poppy and
calendula floating about. Other bits are very patchy, but
if there's some decent rain, I can move things about here
and there. I am quite sure now that there is more light
there'll be more germination too.

Today I must tackle the braced comb, try and find
the queen and set up some measures in preparation
for a swarm because we have many queen cells. I'm
so daunted by the prospect of all of this.

I endlessly message my friend Owen, who keeps a top bar
hive in Cornwall and breeds wonderful and weird plants,
for advice. He's the best sort of friend, pre-empts
everything with 'I've made all the mistakes you can...
try this'.

Steve says to set up a swarm box somewhere and fill it
with comb so that if they do go they might choose that.
He's on a film set coaxing bees somewhere today with Ian
McKellen. Any attempt to discuss finer details ends the
phone call. All I can say is keeping bees is like finding
yourself flying a plane. You know that crashing is the
worst possible outcome, but how you stay up remains a
mystery.

I wouldn't mind if I was around to carry on monitoring,
but I am filming for the next two days and working away
all weekend. It means leaving poor Al to gather the masses
if they go off somewhere else. I wish I'd known that you
really need two hives in the first year to anticipate the
swarm. How did I miss that detail?

On that note Al got stung right in the middle of his head
yesterday. Not entirely sure how, but he seems to be taking
it in good humour.

- A

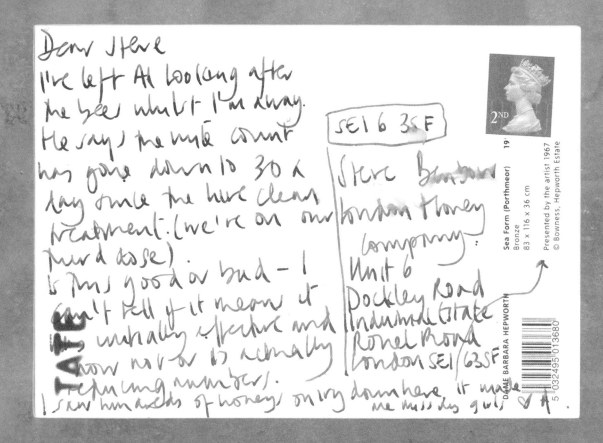

Dear Steve

I've left Al looking after
the bees whilst I'm away.
He says the mite count
has gone down to 30 a
day since the hive clean
treatment. (we're on our
third dose).
Is this good or bad - I
can't tell if it means it
was initially effective and
now no longer is actually
reducing numbers.
I saw hundreds of honeys on my down here. it made
me miss the girls ♡ A

SE1 6 3SF

Steve Benbow
London Honey
Company.
Unit 6
Dockley Road
Industrial Estate
Rotherhithe Road
London SE1 6 3SF

TATE

Sea Form (Porthmeor)
Bronze
83 × 116 × 36 cm

Presented by the artist 1967
© Bowness, Hepworth Estate

2ND
19

DAME BARBARA HEPWORTH

5 032495 013680

11 July

I'm not sure if Alys has spotted her queen yet? It must
be tough trying to spot her anyway this time of year
because the colony is so huge. But even more so with
pancakes of comb and brace, she could hide in numerous
cracks and crevices and elude the viewer. I hear good
things mainly, although I do get a text to say they might
be considering swarming.

I receive a snap of what is a queen cell. The important
thing here is to gauge if it's swarming or super seizure.
In brief, if it's swarming there will be loads of cells,
and if super seizure, where the bees are no longer happy
with the quality of their queen, then just one or two will
appear.

One thought could be that perhaps they are not happy
with the constant attention they are getting and want
out of their manor house.

I try and advise by text. It's hard to know exactly what
is going on but I advise a swarm box, smelling of beeswax,
positioned as high as possible and about ten metres from
the hive entrance.

- S

14 July

Lots of dead young (these are distinctly hairier and paler
- I am proud to say I can finally tell the difference on
that) drones outside the hive. Perhaps 40 or so. I panicked
(predictably).

Me: Al, there are so many dead bees, something terribly
wrong must be happening - they're all going to die.

Al: *immediately starts counting bees* there are 32 dead
bees. In a population of around 30,000, that's less than
0.01%. I don't think that's a problem.

Me: I'm so glad you're good at maths, it's very reassuring.

– A

24 July

It's been a good crop across the country, with some reports
of it being the best on record. If Alys has not been
tearing down combs she should have some honey in the hive
by now from the lime trees that surround the allotment.
Surely Alys – just stop tinkering and let them settle?!

– S

21 August

A blue sort of morning. I wrote emails, wrote lists of
plants I might buy if I owned a different sort of garden,
I visited some pictures of distant mountain views. I
worried about not writing, I worried about worrying about
not writing. I worried.

Then when this worrying had accumulated into a thumping
ball of pressure above my left eye, I went to bed and set
a timer for 20 minutes. An hour and half later I woke in
a pool of dribble, the dull thump still there, as was that
hot sweat from daytime sleep, and I realised that I was
peering down a hole that I was digging. So I went outside
and dug a real one instead.

Steve called. He was passing, but not stopping.
He was fed up with life, life and the bees,
bees and life. But like all his calls, the
shift to other things is quick if you know
where to push. I offered a distraction from
the motorway and took my opportunity to pounce.
I rattled through my questions: is the black
frass on the inspection board below a sign
of wax moth (yes), is spotty laying (pepper
potting is the appropriate term, apparently)
a bad thing (yes, my queen might have exhausted
herself creating such a large colony).

Would I be harvesting honey? No, I am adamant
about that. A crack in the conversation,
I clearly should want to be harvesting honey,
but I jumped it before it could turn into
something else and moved swiftly on to how
to apply HiveClean.

He says he will appear next week.

- A

26 August

My second trip to Birmingham - it's harvest and
fruiting time - which means good trading season,
I'm hoping. Obligatory strong tea is drunk from
various royal commemorative cups. My dog, Teal,
does a pee on the kitchen floor again.

Alys's allotment is a stone's throw away from the house.
What is clearly apparent is that Alys has tended these
bees with the utmost care and devotion. Yes, I think

framed hives, with their structure of adding in more
frames, when required being able to take off honey, are
an easier option, especially for a beginner. But Alys has
made this system work for her through sheer determination
and devotion. Despite the combs being examined for over
40 minutes, the bees remain calm and I even spot some
waggle dancing – communication that there is still
something out there worth foraging on.

We close up the hive and it's produce time. The rules
of swapping appear to have changed; I never just give
away any old honey, but like people to experience a unique
tasting treat. I'm shown around the plot, however, and told
I'm not worthy of specific garlic or some exotic cucumbers.
I protest and say the honey I've arrived with is rather
special and to break out the good stuff or the honeys
are heading back down south. We also cover the back of
the truck with potted foxgloves Alys has been collecting;
the garden is going to love these.

– S

26 August

He appeared.

We went through the hive, which was basically terrifying
for me. Steve pointed out two emerging bees that had
died in their cells with their tongues out. This is
either a sign of starvation or Varroa. My huge colony
turns out to be mostly Italian bees, known for their
love of endless building and brood laying. They've
essentially eaten the best part of their winter stores
already. Our British black honeybee is far more thrifty;
these Italians imagine an endless summer.

I felt a bit heartbroken by this news. I really don't
want to spend the winter feeding them sugar. Still, I
think I probably need to learn to choose my battles a
little more wisely with bee ethics. I'm a hot-headed
beginner still. I get that.

I also apparently don't use enough smoke. I think I sort
of knew that, but tales of over-smoking bees, hell just
keeping the smoker going, sometimes mean that if the
bees are being gentle it's easy to forgo the smoke.

The perceived wisdom is that smoke makes them think
a forest fire is on the way and they gorge themselves
on their honey, ready to take flight. However, I recently
read that this may or may not be true. Smoke masks the
pheromones and stops the bees from sending panic messages.
This makes a lot more sense. Panic one section and the
whole tribe comes to their defence. As Steve pointed
out, gently smoking all the escaping bees as you are
trying to close up the bars makes life much, much easier.
So with smoke I go.

Steve was pretty horrified by our combs, the ones I've been
increasingly proud of. Through new eyes I can see they
rather wobble some. I'm glad he never saw the ones before
them. I had to defend getting rid of anything less than
ruler straight, but I can see his point – next spring I do
need to be ruthless and keep only the best lot so that I
don't go through this whole bracing issue again.

I will say this: he's a very patient man, putting up with
my wild ways. I'm not an easy student, I always challenge
everything and turn immediately left when someone says
right. Poor Steve, I wonder if he realised early on that
I was quite so contrary.

– A

28 August

Dear Ian

I'm sending a ditty to thank you for a nostalgic moment
that occurred in the summer, whilst being the appointed
'Bee Wrangler' on your new film Mr Holmes.

As you opened up the vintage beehive in the orchard
at West Sussex, dressed in your slippers, Panama
hat with elasticated veil and my old antique smoker,
I was instantly swept back to my childhood.

I watched with admiration and affection. In the dappled
light of the warm afternoon I became completely captivated
by the occasion for the scene's duration. For right there
stood my grandfather, with me observing as a small boy,
eager for bee knowledge.

The air was thick as if a bonfire had been lit, from your
bellowing smoker. The bees performed just brilliantly,
going about their business naturally, returning to the
hive with lime pollen and nectar from the ageing estate.
I know it was acting and around you were dozens of
cameras, producers and directors, but I was mesmerised
until I heard the word 'cut'. Then it was back to reality.

A massive thank you also for your substantial honey order,
which I understand is for Christmas treats for friends.

Finally, if you ever desire an afternoon away from it all
on a rooftop in the city with your hands in some calming
bees, then please don't hesitate to give me a call. A hive
awaits those steady hands.

Lot of love,

Stevie

Transported back
in time.
The smokers and
beehives from
this incredible set
reside in our honey
shop in Bermondsey.
But the memory of
this scene will
last forever.

Ian McKellen

2 Se

Ian McKellen

2 September

Try
ma
spil

Wh
Lo
diff

dear Steve

Herewith my contribution to your new honey book. Not very inventive
I'm afraid. The honey I gave to some colleagues on MR HOLMES
was <u>very</u> appreciated.

love   Ian

Ian McKellen

2 September

Try drizzling honey over your granola or onto hot buttered toast or just make a syrup for fresh fruit salad by reducing orange and lemon juice spiked with honey.

When you need a pick-you-up, line up three or four jars from the London Honey Company and dip in your little finger, revelling in the different tastes from the different hives.

Ian McKellen

S: multiple bee stings what a shite day

A: Oh, nature's not playing ball hey?

I can't do much about stings or a lengthy drive home. Other than say when you get here London is sunny and shiny after the deluge and I bet someone will have made supper

And if all else fails ask your dog how much he loves you and I guarantee he'll respond in a gratifying manner. In his eyes the day wasn't wasted at all because it had your company. And in that light there rarely is a bad day...

(OK that's the end of my zen. You could get another job. I'm quite sure you'd make an excellent...)

S: Excellent what?!

A: Drug dealer?

Explorer

Fisherman

Mead revivalist

I think the last one has something to it

S: Pigman

A: But then you'd have to leave your beloved city, unless you wish to change pig laws first

S: You can keep pigs in cities

A: Nope. Not if you want to sell the meat you can't

Anyhow why aren't you going with mead revivalist? It sounds so good

*

A: I have one bee question that doesn't need an immediate answer but I would dearly love your opinion. Are you free at all tomorrow or late today?

S: Ohh that all sounds serious?

A: No, just been reading lots about top bars

*

A: Take no notice of me, I'm just feeling overwhelmed by life at the moment

Oh and I got stung

S: Where?

A: On my finger, so uneventful that it didn't
even turn red. Amazon waterlily prickles are far
worse as far as pain goes

I am learning about how to be a mindful wax
shepherd. Today I was an experimental, slightly
wayward wax shepherd. Next time will be different

*

A: I just saw two bumbles mating - it was amazing
but also weird. Imagine flying and have sex at
the same time. I don't think she was very into
it, she carried on looking for nectar. Or perhaps
that's bee foreplay

Cause he was essentially hitching a ride you
could hear their wings clattering together

I can see I am going to lose this day to
investigating bee sex now

Hope it's not too frantic your end

I'm going to have parsnip honey

S: Pollen!

A: Parsnip pollen. I think fennel pollen is
probably more interesting to eat. Anyhow this is
irrelevant really cause all I want is parsnip
seeds and thanks to the honey I will have plenty.
Meaning less sowing for me to do

*

A: Did you see the honey moon last night?

I love my bees. Mostly because they are the only
ones not robbing the broad beans (Oh boy, do
those bumbles rob fast)

S: Do you think still it's the bumbles that make
the first hole at the back of the flower?

A: Yes, I don't think honeys have big enough
mandibles. Did you know that a bumble is as
likely to bite you as try and sting you?

S: One bit me the other day!

A: Oh I do so love bumbles. You can imagine that
they'd be fun to go to the pub with

S: Yep they would drink a skinful! When are
we off to Devon?!

A: They so would, they'd moonie the honeys and
laugh at their workers' collective mentality

After Italy, beginning of July?

S: OK before the heather moves

*

S: You think you have brace comb problems!

        A: Not good wax shepherding

    *

S: Sorry just filming dancing bees I think you
did well and queen obviously made of resilient
stuff!

        A: Sorry for being a shit beekeeper

S: You're not - I think you are clearly very
passionate and I admire your determination to get
this right. However I'm not sure there is a right
on this as what's right is the bees doing what
the heck they damn want!

    *

S: Lovely article Alys - I'm thinking a visit to
the bees is in order?

        A: We (the honey collective) would love
        that. Also have lots of foxgloves for Tate
        B for you to take back

        *

S: On my way just at start of M40 and deciding if
Teal has eaten some Sudafed tablets! See you soon

        A: Soup is simmering, bread toasting,
        tea brewing, etc...

I once heard of
someone sending
a rugby ball
through the post,
covered in stamps.
I wanted to see if
a runner bean would
arrive if stamped
and posted.

It was refused by
the post office
so I chucked it
in a letter box
and it arrived the
next day to the
gardener — proving
that I also send
letters!

— S

Winding Down

As a Shropshire lad, autumn quickly signified the end of perpetual outdoor summer holidays and this was always bad news. It was usually spent fishing for tiny speckled brook trout or lounging on riverbanks increasing my freckle count.

Vibrant colours and falling leaves signified an increased consumption of soft apples, usually a variety called Blenheim Orange, grown by my grandfather and stored in the autumn in a shed.

Alys's bees relinquished and resigned themselves to uniformity and lost the ability to be creative and freestyle. By the close of autumn, when I last visited, I saw large dinner plates drying on a draining board through the observation window Josh had built. Very few were braced together and out of place.

The cabinet now stored various items of bee paraphernalia: the smoker with a wine cork in its spout to extinguish the smouldering leaves inside. Slightly mildewed protective veils, hive tools and sticky pieces of cardboard covered in oil for the collection of dropped Varroa mites. It looked well-loved and used, and the bees certainly seemed to be prospering.

As for a crop – apparently, there had been one briefly before the rains arrived and now, rightly so, she was hesitant to remove anything this late in the year. But I did sense disappointment. She did want honey in the end!

For a brief period at the end of the summer I understand it was there and in plentiful amounts. Huge combs now devoted to stores, excess amounts I understand were waiting for procurement, except it was left too long as the weather turned and the bees had consumed it by the time cropping commenced.

I explained she had paid a price for gentle, forgiving bees that had a tendency to build large colonies in the autumn. It meant there were large numbers to feed and the colony had become hungry during damp, cold conditions.

Perhaps then it was time for an upgrade in her second year of beekeeping: a bee that was less forgiving, a bee that would deal with life and production a little differently. The temperament would be different, but a smaller autumn nest and thrifty eater would mean more of a chance of honey removal for personal use.

She had started keeping bees for their welfare and the pollination of the allotments, which was terrific, and I certainly agree she was devoted and dedicated to their every whim. In fact, more dedicated and devoted than I was to the care of the garden at the Tate.

In my defence, I was told in the spring that it should never need watering, and if it did, the garden was not operating correctly. Only to be told months later in the summer that it was now dying and 'why had I not been watering it?'

Perhaps my hopes for the garden were unrealistic: I expected instant results and for seeds to spring into life in a matter of weeks, developing into lush blooms for all to admire and their fine nectar reaped.

STEVE'S THOUGHTS...

As autumn tumbled into view, the bees were still busy, mostly being huge. The queen it seemed had no sense of the impending weather and her colony ate through their honey with what felt like glee. Steve came and visited and declared that they would have to be fed over the winter. My heart sank. I have a deep distrust of white sugar and now I had a huge workforce relying on me to ply them with the stuff.

There's a nuanced argument here for native honeybees. Importing in bees with a gentle nature or a capacity to build large colonies makes for easier conventional beekeeping, but there is something to be said for a bee that understands the season coming up, however feisty.

Visiting the bees has a lovely rhythm to it and I enjoyed immensely pondering at their world, but I did feel a huge sense of failure that we had absolutely no honey to show for our efforts.

Still, it remains a thrill to visit them and one I hope I never lose. Varroa, wax moths, sugar supplements, brace combs: that hive threw everything at us and yet I never truly wanted to walk away. Beekeeping is an endless, very beautiful riddle – a brilliant dilemma; a philosophical and ethically challenging

test, an issue that requires careful handling and at some point I hope a jar of honey or two.

Whilst the bees challenged me, the garden at the Tate vexed me. I was just too far away to keep on top of it. I felt there were too many critics, all impatient for an instant garden, when I knew that if it was to work I had to leave it up to the soil. That's why sowing from seed is such an important tool in these sorts of spaces: it's cheap and you can sow a variety of species, which means something will work, even if it's not quite what you expected. All seeds have a set of cogs that allows germination to occur and each species has its own pattern for how those cogs needs to be set in motion.

Seed only germinates when it is ready and this might be a slower route, but it's one that is resolutely sensible and sustainable. Still people kept turning up to weed, even if they did think the whole garden was merely made of nettles.

> 'Beekeeping is an endless, very beautiful riddle – a brilliant dilemma'

ALYS'S THOUGHTS...

159

2 September

Spent the day at Tate Britain gardening. Much to my
delight and surprise, word had got out amongst the
staff and a great gang appeared at lunchtime. They were
a brilliant, witty bunch who worked hard on the weeds and
despite a few disparaging comments, on the whole I think
the meadow is turning the corner. This dry, dry summer
hasn't helped much, but a second wave of germination has
occurred and another will come in spring if we can keep
on top of the nettles. We at least have a wonderful rich
compost pile in the making.

Steve brought young foxgloves, alchemilla and granny's
bonnets from the allotment so that I could supplement
some gaps. Then this autumn, when it really rains and
the soil is damp, I'll split some of the great clumps
of foxgloves that have already sprung so there's a more
even distribution. Still I am quietly confident that next
summer it will look good and hopefully we can build on
it from there.

I keep promising myself that I'll carefully negotiate
my way out of this one because it doesn't make sense
to travel so far, but then I think about that sweep
of blooms and how nice it will be if you come around
an unexpected corner of the gallery and find something
wild and I realise I'll never quite get out of this one.

I left Steve to water again. He promises he will. I'm not
sure quite why I keep falling for that ruse.

  - A

15 September

We re-sow the Tate and plant with hundreds of allotment
foxgloves I'm told to water, so I choose the nighttime,
as it's the only time I have at the moment. Security there
are puzzled but they have seen me there at numerous times
across the summer and are not that surprised by my
midnight foray.

- S

26 September

The weather has been kind to the bees, who have been
hard at work putting honey down. Interestingly they haven't
touched the fondant, proving that flowers are better than
white sugar.

We removed a few more frames that were only half-built
or too crazily built, so that we now have twelve or so
fairly straight, fairly standard frames, all with space
to add more honey if the month allows. Still Varroa around,
we keep dousing them in hippy juice and they keep falling
off. Strange thing is, as hard as I look on the combs
I can never find a single bee with a Varroa stuck on.

I get a sinking feeling about this winter and the bees.
I hope they are well enough to make it through. The recent
increase in honey is pleasing – most combs are capped
to at least three quarters of the way down, so I hope
that's enough.

I was cleaning up my office when I found the first frame
I built at beekeeping night classes. National frames are
tiny compared to the size of my top bar combs, which are
almost three times the size. Who knows if this is a good
or bad thing, but I have to remember when I run into other
beekeepers and they boast proudly of their mountains of
jars that my hive has honey. It's just where it should be.

I run from being slightly irritated that the bees have
produced so much brood and so much comb to great shame
that I let them. I realise my poor bees have spent most
of the year making wax. I should be training to become
a candle maker. (Al and I have hatched a Christmas present
plan for this.)

These poor bees. I took all my amateurish ideas and
inexperience out on them. Then, when I didn't have liquid
gold to wave under everyone else's nose (even Steve has
asked me at least half a dozen times about harvesting and
he's seen inside), I felt ashamed, like I had failed at the
first hurdle.

The strangest thing about all of this is that it's rather
put me off eating honey. I have a cupboard full of the
stuff that I have bought or have been gifted and I barely
touch it.

- A

Closing Up

24/1

Dear Alys

EMORSGATESEEDS
Foxglove
Digitalis purpurea
Origin: *Suffolk*
Contents: 10g
Packed: February 2014   14-1-21

24/1   ①

Dear Alys

It Was Incredible   to s
your allotment bees to da
on my Way back from chec
nine in Shropshire!
The bees that gathered the
heather honey from the Long
Mynd are now back amongst
coppicing of the country Estat
until the late spring.
Their roofs were covered in sno
and the pheasants had been usi

them as perches,
hive entrance
blocks had to

EMORSGATESEEDS
Rough Chervil
Chaerophyllum temulum
Origin: *Oxfordshire*
Contents: 10g
Packed: February 2014   03-1-11

mice from coming in and chewin
homes of wax. Something I a
sure   Won't happen with you
hive as it is situated at such he

② However...

③ I'm delighted

don't know if you were in a hurry in the middle of something else hen I arrived but the bee inspection at was conducted was rather eeting?

had only just arrived and the hive of was already off and you were rting to begin an examination! Was so rushed and intense - no a or chat, just straight into them and caught me completely on the hop. iked to be prepared and sorted before

EMORSGATE**S**EEDS

Ramsons

Allium ursinum

Origin: Pembrokeshire
Contents: 10g
Packed: February 2014   02-1-21

a smoker lit?

's also good to spend a few minutes the front of the hive, before you art, to see if there are bees flying in with pollen.

to see the strong bond you have built with them across the seasons. Where as I believed you could just let a garden get on with it, you have fully devoted your spare time to your bee's welfare.

I hear there is talk of expansion this year with another hive, that perhaps is a little more straight forward and on frames.

From the view window Josh build for you, I saw the most perfect looking

pancakes hanging down

EMORSGATE**S**EEDS

Wood Sage

Teucrium scorodonia

Origin: Suffolk
Contents: 20g
Packed: February 2014   07-1-31

from their top bars.

I know these have not come easily and I don't think I would have had the determination and discipline you have shown.

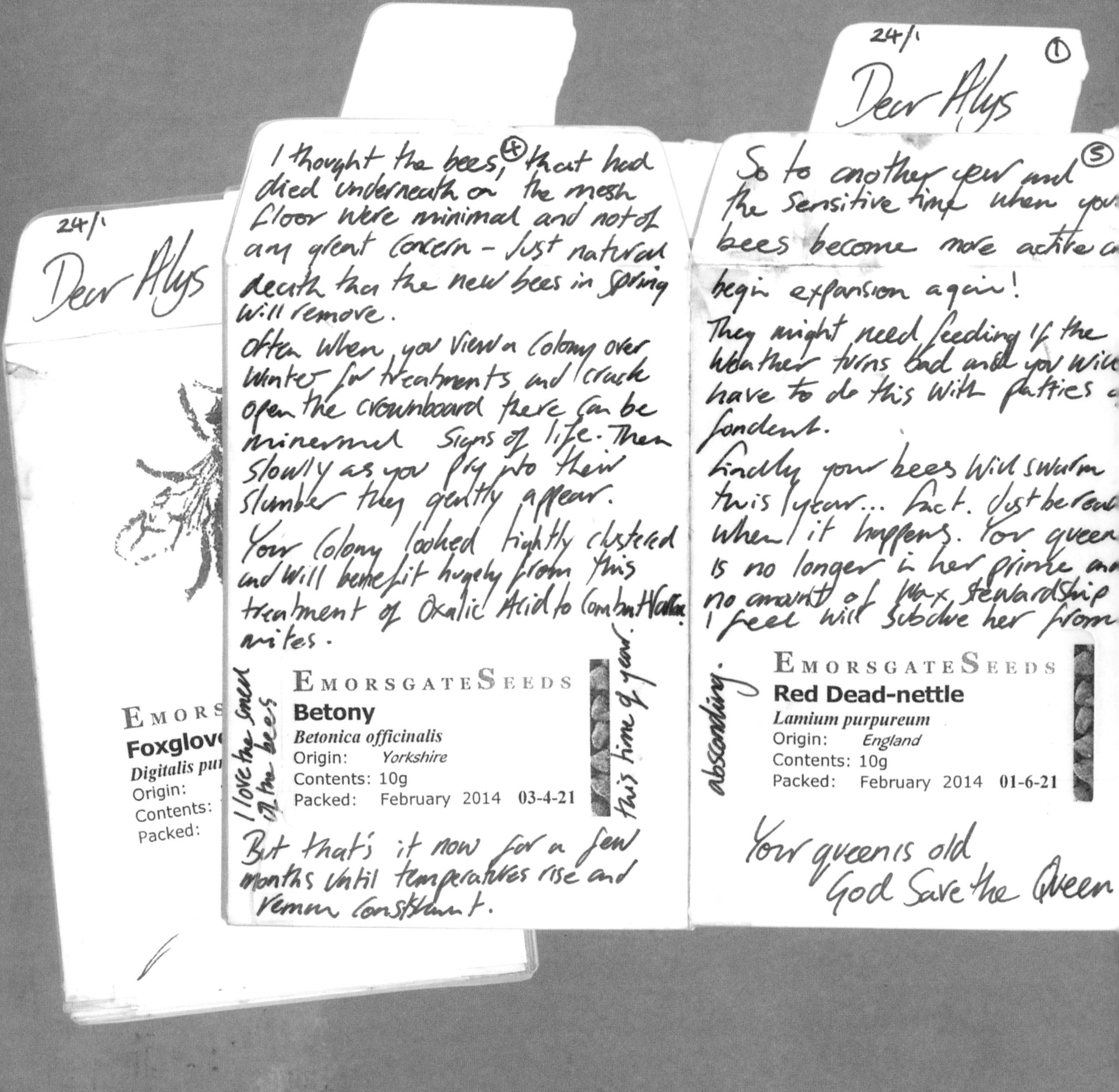

24/1

Dear Alys

Emors
Foxglove
Digitalis pur
Origin:
Contents:
Packed:

(4) I thought the bees, that had died underneath on the mesh floor were minimal and not of any great concern – just natural death that the new bees in spring will remove.

Often when you view a colony over winter for treatments and crack open the crownboard there can be minimal signs of life. Then slowly as you pry into their slumber they gently appear.

Your colony looked tightly clustered and will benefit hugely from this treatment of Oxalic Acid to combat Varroa mites.

I love the smell of the bees

Emorsgate Seeds
Betony
Betonica officinalis
Origin: Yorkshire
Contents: 10g
Packed: February 2014 03-4-21

this time of year.

But that's it now for a few months until temperatures rise and remain constant.

24/1 (1)

Dear Alys

(5) So to another year and the sensitive time when your bees become more active and begin expansion again!

They might need feeding if the weather turns bad and you will have to do this with patties or fondant.

Finally your bees will swarm this year... fact. Just be ready when it happens. Your queen is no longer in her prime and no amount of wax stewardship I feel will subdue her from absconding.

Emorsgate Seeds
Red Dead-nettle
Lamium purpureum
Origin: England
Contents: 10g
Packed: February 2014 01-6-21

Your queen is old
God Save the Queen

②
However...

③
I'm delighted

⑥
PS

know if you were in
e middle of something
I arrived the
as const

hanks for the
nazing garden.
hink it will flourish this year
d the bees — bumbles, honeys
solitary will love it.

nwards and upwards and I
pe one day we can create a
arden boat that can be moored
the Thames for Chelsea
lower Show?

have
he seasons.
al just
it, you
e time

nsion
e, that
ht forward

ild for
ct looking

from their
top buds.

easily
re had

re you

With
Jane Stem

EMORSGATESEEDS
Wild Carrot
Daucus carota ssp carota
Origin: *Hertfordshire*
Contents: 1g
Packed: February 2014   08-4-21

EMORSGATESEEDS
Nettle-leaved Bellflower
Campanula trachelium
Origin: *Somerset*
Contents: 10g
Packed: February 2014   02-2-31

As I write, I'm warm, dry and clean and look out onto the most glorious of tiny London gardens in the heart of Hackney. Life is certainly better than it has been, when I was nomadic and on the road with my bees a few years ago.

I do miss the ambling and the bumbling, the not knowing and the constant migration. But my business has become established now and this allows more consistency of life. Yes, there are the stresses of running a business and I do miss the freedom and carefree lifestyle I had. But I now have a dog and own a washing machine. I'm totally domesticated, me.

I've been very fortunate. I have found someone who loves me and a new friend for life. It just so happens they are two different people but there is nothing wrong with that. Alys has become my new best friend, who I consult with on a variety of matters, not just gardening.

The garden actually came to fruition the following spring and what a picture it looked when it eventually did bloom in all its glory. Alys had weakened under the weight of my constant misgivings and we added extra foxgloves from her allotment. There was a little bit more seed scattering but I had not really quite anticipated how incredible it would actually become.

The crescendo arrived as the crab apple blooms burst out during an unusually warm spring, which saw record temperatures allowing for a long flowering session and cow parsley grew taller than myself. It seemed to be mainly the colour of purple.

Then there were the insects. Of course I became exited when I saw my own bees frequenting the takeaway honesty flowers but I counted over five types of native bees and numerous hoverflies. Bumblebees disappeared for what appeared to be minutes in the rotund foxgloves tubes, the complete bell vibrating to a merry dance on closer inspection.

Was it all a success? God, no. Would I like to repeat it and could I build a garden of my own? Well, I like to feel I've attempted it in my own yard and we plan to make some planters out of old honey barrels for the front of the railway arches which we have recently moved our bee business into.

Long and thin, it's similar to a top bar hive. In the middle is the nest of the production and honey-packing rooms and on the fringes the barrels of honey gathered from our resourceful and incredible bees from around the UK.

– Steve

STEVE'S THOUGHTS...

Nature was on my side. The following year the whole garden burst into song, and thickets of foxgloves, sweet rocket, frothy umbels, poppies, calendula and mallows appear in a great crescendo. Steve called up and said the thing all gardeners long to hear, that the garden looked beautiful, and the only thing a beekeeping gardener needs to hear, that it was full of the sounds of happy insects.

We met, two years on from our funny introduction and sat in our garden, looking at our flowers, discussing our bees, and when I cycled off, I wondered if our friendship was bound by this book. When I first met Steve he was wild: he lived a nomadic, often erratic, life chasing bees. By the time our garden flowered, he had been gently tamed by love and was domesticated in a good way, the way of a good garden, loved and managed and still space for something wild. And I, on the other hand, had swapped roles; his bees had given me flight and desire to see over the fence to go further than my ordinary boundaries. The bees have driven me a little wild, but that, as they say, is for another story.

If there is one thing that Steve has truly taught me it's that honey is a precious resource that shouldn't be squandered. When you open up a good jar of honey, go slowly. Take in the aroma for there is no smell that captures summer better. Take a tiny dip and sink into the flora of wherever it has come from. Note how the honey changes as you linger over it; there are citrus notes, pine notes, aniseed and mint.

Some honeys are made for cheese, others to go straight on good bread with nothing in-between, some are to skate over butter and others to swirl into cool yoghurt. Rarely is a good honey improved by cooking with it, because heat destroys all that is special and healthful about it. Honey and beeswax is magical stuff and does wonderful things for us, but it doesn't mean that they should be found willy-nilly in any old product.

This morning I dipped my spoon into a strange and exotic honey from Zambia that Steve is importing and I sent Steve a text asking him how to tackle my ever-increasing colony. I have survived another season as a beekeeper and I know this much: the bees and I are sticking together.

I predict he'll be quite the gardener someday. I hope he thinks the same about my beekeeping.

– Alys

Letters & Postcards

Beginning
Pages 16–17

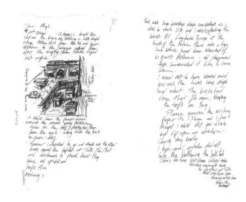

Dear Alys.

29th October – 16 degrees C bright blue sky and the bees
are dashing in with bright orange pollen still from the
Ivy and seem oblivious to the Carnage around them, after
the mighty storm which raged last night.

Nov 3rd

It would seem the parapit which surrounds the small young
polishing hives on the roof protected them from the gails
– along with the brick on each roof.

However I decided to go and check all the other hives
around the Capital at Tate Mod/Brit and Fortnums to
check that they were all upright and safe this morning.

There were huge branches down everywhere as I drove to
each site and I was expecting the worst. At Lambeth Bridge
at the back of the Palace there was a huge limb which hand
been wrenched of giant Acacia – red chequered tape
surrounded it like a crime scene.

I need not to have worried mind you all the hives were
upright and intact. The bricks had done their job again,
keeping the roofs on.

Please excuse the writing paper its 1.36am and I just
thought I would drop you a note and rip open an envelope
- Clearly very badly.

I hope your garden did not take the battering the South
took. Clearly we have lost some valued nectar sources
overnight here. So Garden at Tate must crack on soon.
Running out of room.

Yours the beekeeper

Beginning
Pages 18–19

14th December

Dearest Ben,

I've spent all day waiting for the scaffolders to come and
take down their poles etc, I've been pacing up and down
the house like some caged animal. Every two seconds back
to the garden and then to the front door (I missed them
the last time). And there between stretches I saw her a
great huge fat Bombus terrestris queen, so large that you'd
hardly believe she could fly.

Buff-tail are supposed to be very fond of Arbutus unedo,
the strawberry tree. It flowers from now into December,
tiny white bells like bell heather, that if the weather
is mild are often followed by the strawberry-like fruit.

The species name unedo means 'eat only once' as Pliny
thought them tasteless.

In Spain the fruit are fermented into an alcoholic
concoction that I always fantasize I'll make one day.
Still it's very pleasing to find her dinning on my tree.

I chased her around the garden only to hear the scaffolders
knocking and then had to leave her be.

I love those fat queens, how can something so heavy fly?
She defies logic. I hope she comes back again soon.

Now that the scaffolding is gone I am off to plant yet
more bulbs.

Speak soon,

Alys

Beginning
Page 20-23

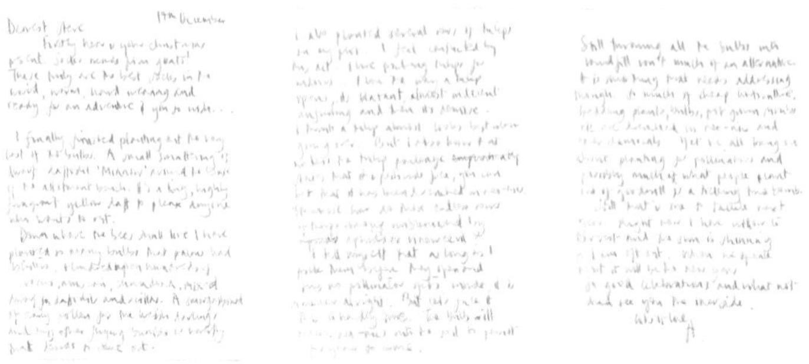

17th December

Dearest Steve

Firstly here is your christmas present. Socks made from goats! These truly are the best socks in the world; warm, hard wearing and ready for an adventure if you so wish...

I finally finished planting out the very last of the bulbs. A small smattering of dwarf daffodil 'Minnow' around the base of the allotment bench. It's a tiny, highly fragrant yellow daff to please anyone who wants to rest.

Down where the bees shall live I have planted so many bulbs that palms had blisters. Hundred upon hundreds of crocus, muscari, chionodoxa, mixed dwarf daffodils and scillas. A smorgasboard of early pollen for the welsh darling and any other flying bumble or hoverfly that decide to come out.

I also planted several rows of tulips on my plot. I feel conflicted by this act. I love picking tulips for indoors. I love the way a tulip opens, its blatant, almost indecent unfurling and then its demise. I think a tulip almost

looks best when going over. But I also know that unless
the tulip package ~~emphatically~~ states that it is pesticide
free, you can bet that it has been drenched in neo-nics.
Otherwise how do those endless rows of tulips come up
unblemished by aphids or vineweevil?

I tell myself that as long as I pick them before they
open and thus no pollinator gets inside, it is somehow
alright. But let's face it this is hardly true. The bulb
will release neo-nics into the soil to persist for years
to come.

Still throwing all the bulbs into landfill isn't much
of an alternative. It is something that needs addressing
though. So much of cheap horticulture bedding plants,
bulbs, pot grown shrubs, etc are drenched in neo-nics
and other chemicals. Yet we all bang on about planting
for pollinators and possibly much of what people plant
out of goodwill is a ticking time bomb.

Still that is one to tackle next year. Right now I have
willow to harvest - and the sun is shining so I am oft
out. When we speak next it will be the new year.

So good celebrations and what not and see you the other
side.

Lots of love

A.

Getting Ready
Pages 52–55

21st February
Birmingham

Dear Ben,

I saw my first bumble of the season on Wednesday.
So it starts, it means it's happening again. I always
worry slightly that I have dreamt spring up.

I'd received a surprise package of plants from a nursery
and in it was a Hellebore 'Candy Love' in full flower,
a lovely gift if ever there was one. It's flowers start
off a delicate ivory and with age gradually deepen to
a blush pink before fading to a dusty chocolate purple.
The most graceful aging you can imagine.

It takes time to know where a plant should sit, you
can't just go out and plant it straight into the ground.
I leave it in its pot and then try it out in various
locations till I find the one that suits it and me best.
And whilst I was pondering the merits of a site, there
the buff-tailed bumble buzzed in. That it chose to dine
on a recent rhododendron rather than the full buffet
of other hellebores, snowdrops, primroses and Eranthis

I'd laid out for it was, I guess, neither here nor there.
I pretended not to be hurt. 'Candy Love' is as its name
suggests clearly intoxicating.

It was heartening to see a bumble, to smell the earth
sweetening and see the dull winter greens recede
as the new growth stirs. Of course its bitter again,
the ground solid and the wind whips through you. I am
staying inside and sowing seeds. February is running
away and the windowsills are beginning to burgeon with
seedlings. H mutters darkly about this takeover. I guess
he knows in a month or so he loses me to the garden again
and these seedlings represent that March.

I hope the bitter winds didn't spoil Cornwall? Did you
brave the sea?

I'm in London editing next week so I might try and drop
by for a refill of honey (can I bring my own jars?) Do you
want anything from the garden? There's limited choice
winter salads with chicories (tasting perfect, the frost
has just taken off their bitter edge), cabbage, potatoes
or Jerusalem artichokes (mountains off them, I promise
to put winter savoy in this time).

Alys x

<u>Getting Ready</u>
<u>Page 57</u>

Dear Alys

What an enlightening visit to Buckfast.

Instead of bee breeding and colossal honey production,
today they are focused on bee education and this
is very much prevalent amongst the local community.

They are also undergoing field trials of a predatory mite
which feeds off adult Varroa mites across the summer,
which sounds fantastic, and I'm keen to try them on
myown bees here in the smoke.

The Barefoot Beekeeper was also only a short drive down
the road at Totnes. We met in a local pub and drank
buckets of tea.

I'm intrigued by his 'Eco floor' which trys to replicate
the base of a hollow tree and the bees natural habitat
and I think is worth a try on your own Top Bar Hive?

Season about to start here as warm days forecasted
lots of love
S

Planting
Pages 84–85

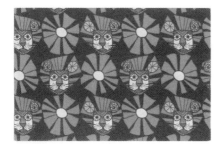 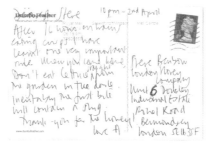

10pm – 2nd April

Dearest Steve

After 16 hours on trains eating crisps I have learnt one
very important rule: When you come home, Don't eat lettuce
straight from the garden in the dark. Inevitably the first
bite will contain a slug.

Thank-you for the honey!

Love A.

Planting
Pages 92-95

19th April

Ben

I wanted to tell you this, but somewhere in that slightly
sad conversation about failed avenues and lost queens,
I felt too shy to say it.

Last week at the university, whilst teaching outside I came
across a bee on the floor. The hives had been buzzing all
morning and I knew that if I left her there she would most
likely get squashed as she sat on the path to the potting
shed.

So I picked her up and looked around for something
to please her. All I could think of was to offer up
some water. I dipped one muddy hand into the watering
can and made a small well of water in my palm.
A distinctly earthy drink, but something never the
lessand then I carefully transferred her from one palm
to the other.

She drank and very meticulously washed her face and
antennae.

I stared so hard and so close so that I could see every
detail. And only when I was an eye ball away from her did
it occur to me that she was staring back just as hard.
And there we stood looking at each other's strangeness.

And then, I felt her murmur, her whole body vibrate and
for a second my heart missed a beat, had I made her angry?
And like that she was gone, high up into the sky.

That moment when you feel the engine start up, like
an old mower humming and buzzing into action is really
quite something.

Those precious seconds before flight – that is what
I wanted to tell you about. That I felt the moment
and I felt as alive as she did.

Lots of love

A.

Feeding
Pages 120–121

Perhaps we should plant trees here?

Dear Beekeeper

Fill seed tray with good quality PEAT-FREE seed compost.

Carefully place seed ontop on compost and lightly firm
in (do not bury them in more compost). Cover the seed
with a thin layer of grit or sand. Light seems to play
a part in germination so <u>do not</u> bury them too deep.

Sit tray in water until the top is damp – take out of water
– and place in a clear plastic bag. Put in fridge for 1
week. Remove to sunny windowsil @ 21°C (keep clear plastic
bag on until you see seeds appear. CROSS FINGERS.

Flowering
Pages 128-129

I will say this much about beekeeping so far. Its lonely,
sad, demoralising, crushing, but mostly heart-breaking.

I think I've found the one thing I can't survive.
Most though I just feel lost.

love me sad novice.

Flowering
Page 132–133

A little erotic floral photography never goes amiss
in a man's life.

I'm off to Italy, I will return in a week. Meet at Tate
Britain, say Thursday or Friday to do some weeding.
Am happy to go alone if you are too busy, but as always
your company makes it far more enjoyable.

♥ A

Flowering
Pages 138–139

Dear Steve

I've left Al looking after the bees whilst I'm away.
He says the mite count has gone down to 30 a day since
the hive clean treatment. (we're on our third dose).

Is this good or bad – I can't tell if it means it was
initially effective and now not or is actually reducing
numbers.

I saw hundreds of honeys on ivy down here, it made me
miss my girls

♥ A

Closing Up
Pages 166–169

24/1

(1) Dear Alys

It was incredible to see your allotment bees today
on my way back from checking mine in Shropshire.

The bees that gathered the heather honey from the Long
Mynd are now back amongst the coppicing of the Country
Estate until the late spring.

Their roofs were covered in snow and the pheasants
had been using them as perches. Hive entrance blocks

had to be replaced and wedged in with twigs to prevent
mice from coming in and chewing frames of wax. Something
I am sure won't happen with your hive as it is situated
at such height.

(2) However...
I don't know if you were in a hurry or in the middle
of something else when I arrived but the bee inspection
that was conducted was rather fleeting?

I had only just arrived and the hive roof was already
off and you were starting to begin an examination! It was
so rushed and intense - no tea or chat, just straight into
them and it caught me completely on the hop. I liked to
be prepared and sorted before I open a hive, at least have
a smoker lit?

It's also good to spend a few minutes at the front of the
hive, before you start, to see if there are bees flying
in with pollen.

(3) I'm delighted

to see the strong bond you have built with them across
the seasons. Where as I believed you could just let
a garden get on with it, you have fully devoted your
spare time to your bee's welfare.

I hear there is talk of expansion this year with another
hive, that perhaps is a little more straightforward and
on frames.

From the view window Josh built for you, I saw the most
perfect looking pancakes - hanging down from their top
bars. I know these have not come easily and I don't think
I would have had the determination and discipline you
have shown.

(4) I thought the bees that had died underneath on the
mesh floor were minimal and not of any great concern –
Just natural death that the new bees in spring
will remove.

Often when you view a colony over winter for treatments
and crack open the crownboard there can be minermal signs
of life. Then slowly as you pry into their slumber they
gently appear.

Your colony looked tightly clustered and will benefit
hugely from this treatment of Oxalic Acid to combat Varroa
mites.

I love the smell of the bees this time of year.

But that's it for now for a few months until temperatures
rise and remain consistent.

(5) So to another year and the sensitive time when your
bees become more active and begin expansion again!

They might need feeding if the weather turns bad and you
will have to do this with patties of fondant.

Finally your bees will swarm this year... fact. Just be
ready when it happens. Your queen is no longer in her
prime and no amount of wax stewardship I feel will subdue
her from absconding.

Your queen is old

God Save the Queen

(6) PS

Thanks for the amazing garden. I think it will flourish
this year and the bees - bumbles, honeys and solitary
will love it.

Onwards and upwards and I hope one day we can create
a garden boat that can be moored on the Thames for
Chelsea Flower Show?

With love

Steve

ABOUT THE AUTHORS

···

Steve Benbow runs the London Honey Company, which he set up in 1999 from the roof of an ex-council block in Tower Bridge. It now has hives on the roof of Fortnum and Mason, Tate Modern and the National Portrait Gallery. Random House published his first book, *The Urban Beekeeper*, in 2012.

Alys Fowler is a gardener who loves food. She is the author of several books, writes a weekly column on gardening for *Guardian Weekend* magazine and presents gardening programmes on TV (including her own show *The Edible Garden*). She lives in Birmingham and enjoys wild swimming, riding bikes and cooking.

ACKNOWLEDGEMENTS
...

We would like to thank Lucy and her wonderful team at Holmes Wood for making this book so beautiful; to everyone who scattered seeds and pulled weeds at Tate Britain; to the top bar beekeepers online and afar who helped resolve a wonky comb and offered words of encouragement.

Plenty has changed in our world since we first started writing this book together, many years ago. I now live in a delightful dwelling, and that's thanks to a very loving partner who decided to house a vagrant and his dog! So, huge love and warmth to Aileen and sorry for the clutter, sticky dog and strewn bee overalls.

I would also like to thank my bees, for their solace and devotion, and the team at The London Honey Company.

To Juliet and Neil for helping with our crowdfunding film, to all those at Unbound and to our supporters who stuck with us to see this book come to fruition. But mostly to all the hard-working pollinators who we chased, cajoled, peered and wondered at.

– Steve

Thank you to Birgit and Nick, Sue and Les, Ingrid and Jeremy, Al and Kat, Owen, Emily Reed, the top bar community online and afar, Fionnuala and family, all at Ballymaloe, Clare, Emily, Dave, Ming and Sarah. To the rescue party that came to Tate Britain to pull weeds. To the many others that helped at Tate Britain, Juliet and Neil, Jonny and Becca, Mum and Dad. And to Ben!

– Alys

SUPPORTERS

...

Unbound is a new kind of publishing house. Our books are funded directly by readers. This was a very popular idea during the late eighteenth and early nineteenth centuries. Now we have revived it for the internet age. It allows authors to write the books they really want to write and readers to support the books they would most like to see published.

    The names listed below are of readers who have pledged their support and made this book happen. If you'd like to join them, visit www.unbound.com.

Philippa A
John Adams
Marilyn Adams
Julie Addis
Ben Addy
James Alexander-Sinclair
Hannah Allan
Rob Amour
Karen Anagnos
Ella Ancheta
Meredith Andrew
Vicki Angus
annefairbrother
John Annett
Eike Armbrust
Penny Arrowood
Megan Ashfield
Daphne Astor
Elliott Atkinson
Richard Atkinson
Vivien Atkinson
Lizi Attwood &
  Ross Mansfield
Helen Axe
Duncan Baird
Georgina Baker
Julie Baker

Melanie Baker
Nicola Balakian
Katherine Baldock
Jennifer Ball
Dineke Barendrecht
Diana Barker
Julia Barnhouse
Alison Bartlett
Ruth Barton
Helen Bates
Kristin Bathurst
Belinda Bauer
Samuel Becker
James Bedding
Cindi Bedor
Sue Beesley
Gordon Bell
Lucy Bellamy
Carolyn Belson
John Benbow
Caroline Bendall
Michelle Best
Katja Gliha Betz
Nick Bingham
Martin Blacher
Judy Blackett
Monique Borst

Keir Bosley
Jacqueline Boston
Sarah Bowyer
Benjamin Brace
Susan Bradley
Naomi Bradshaw
Gwenda Braid
Victoria Brandon
David Brimble
Andy Broadhurst
Stewart Bromfield
Manda Brookman
Emma Brown
Martin Brown
Michael Brown
Julie Bruggeman
Gareth Buchaillard-Davies
Lisa Buckley
Anne Bufton
Monika Bulsiewicz
Andrea Burden
David Burgess
Sarah Burgess
Jeremy Burke
Kerry Burke
Peter Bustin
Eddy Butcher

The Butchery Ltd
Guy E N Buxton
Stephen Byrne
Ian Callaghan
Julie Campbell
Marion Campbell
Xander Cansell
Amanda Carr
Mike Carver
Emily Casstles
Jeannette Caswell
Matthew Caton
Phil Chandler
Bob Bob Chapman
Michelle Chapman
Pete Chapman
Jon Chase
Yvanna Chase
George Chelton
Stella Chevalier
Chunk
Fiona Clark
Jim Clark
Linda Clark
James Clarkson
Linda Clarkson
Pete Clasby
Viki Clegg
Katherine Clifton
Nick Clifton-Welker
Neil Clowes
Ken Coello
Deborah Colella
Pat Colledge
Bernie & Michael Connor
Aylie Cooke
Louise Cooke
Stephen Cooke
Sarah Coomer
Sally Anne Cooney
Emma Cooper
Fiona Cooper

Robert Cooper
Simon Cornwell
Yvonne Cosgrove
Winter Cournane-Ward
Ann Coyne
Harriet Craig
Julia Craik & The Bee-
    Friendly Seed Partnership
Peter Crangle
Rose Creeser
Sarah Crowson
Desiree Cuatt
Aidan Cuffe
David Cummings
Anthony Cunningham
Louise Curley
Henrik Dahle
Catherine Daly
Mary Dass
Suzanne Davidson
Abbe Davies
Graham Davies
Jasmine Davies
Sara Davison
Ming de Nasty &
    Sarah Tiptoe Girl
Rachel de Thample
Paul Debois
Líadain Decken
Benny Declerck
Aaron Deemer
Nik Veselyevich Demented
Alice Denford
Judith Dennison
Mark Diacono
Joanna Dobson
Julius Domoney
Kate Donohoe
Jillian Dougan
Helena Dove
Lawrence T Doyle
Rebecca Doyle

Ciara Dudleston
David Duffy
Jane Dutton
Ben Dwyer
Rachel Dye
Tony Dymond
Kelly Eardley
Judy Earl
Mag. Dr. Helgo Eberwein
Anna Egger
Glynis Eley
J. B. Elgar
Tom Elliott
Nathan Evans
evilgordon
Susan Fallon
Rebecca Falvey
Wayne Farrell
Virginia Fassnidge
Joycelyn & Peter Faulkner
David Fé
Tamar Feast
Elsie Fecher
Agnes Ferwerda
Susannah Field
Sue Fielding
Bill Fitzmaurice
Jasmin Ford
Colin Forrest-Charde
David James Fort
Elizabeth Fowler
Jonathan Fowler
Magali Fowler
Isobel Frankish
Jan Fuscoe
Erika Gard
Laura Gardner
Phil Gatley
Pamela Gatrell
Paul Geary
Marc Gellatly
Aileen Geraghty

Ben Geraghty
Cara Geraghty
Conor Geraghty
Helen Geraghty
John Geraghty
Oliver Geraghty
Thierry Gerber
Lauren & Mark Giannullo
Trish Gibson
Adam Gill
Toni Gill
Vicky Gillibrand
Karen Gimson
Helen Gladman
Sukie Gladstone
Margaret Gleeson
Rosy Glover &
  Jonathan Tritton
Thomas Godfrey
Sophie Goldsworthy
Edmund Gooch
Samantha Goodlet
Lizzie Gordon
Vicky Gorry
Yve Grace
Joanna Gradwell
Ian Grainger
Rachel Gray
Lorna Green
Rebecka Gullstrand
Kevin Gumienny
Theo Gwyther
Stephen J Hackett
William Hackett-Jones
Deborah Haffenden
James Haliburton
Ben and Freya Hall
Gillian Hall
Lucy Hall
Nick Harbour
Lisa Hardi
Jarret Hardie

Michael Hardman
Tina Harper
Karen Harries
Letitia Harris
Nikki Harris
Beth Harrison
Kerry Harrison
Kris James Harrison
Caroline Hart
Beckii Harvey
Caitlin Harvey
Ed Harvey
Maddie Harvey
Sally Harvey
Lyndsey Haskell
Tanya Hawkes
Richard Hawley
Joanne Haywood
Patricia Healey
Andrew Hearse
Gerry Heaton
Dan Heaver
Tim Henderson
Christine Herne
Nici Hewitson
Diana Heyer
Anna Higgins
higgledygarden.com
Sarah Hill
Adam Hindle
Michelle Hiscutt
Adrianne Hlavenka
Rachel Hodge
Mark Hodgson
Fellow urban beekeeper
  John Holland
Lucy Holmes
Sarah Holyoake
The Honeymakers
Sandie Hope
Christine Hopkins
Ann Horne

Robin Hoshino
Anabel Hudson
Dawn Hunter
Lee Hurst
Alison Hutchison
Jake Huzel
Deb Ikin
Holiday Inn
Catherine Innes
intoGardens
Mark Jago
Bonnie James
Lotte Janssens
Katja Jassey
Paul and Sara Jenkins
Zoe Olivia John
Wendy Johnson
Aideen & Denis Jones
Dorothy Jones
Terry Jones
Nicholas Jordan
Martina Karlsson
Sue Kaye
Gerry Keane
Erik Kearney
Lynn Keddie
Alice Keen
Charlotte Keen
Birgit Kehrer
Gert Keiner with
  birthday greetings from
  your English friends
Lindsey Kemp
Laura Kennedy-Rankin
Sally Kent
Amanda Kerr
Katie Kerr
George Khayat
Dan Kieran
Helen Kindness
Ele King
Jennifer King

Joe King
Susie King
Michael Kinghan
Daniel Kleinman
Britta Klemm
Jon Knight
Julie Knight
Lisajane Koea
Janet Kreysa
Ian & Susan Lacey
Laura & Ollie Lambert
Jo Lambkin
Ian Lancaster
Susan Lanfear
Faye Langston
Ian Larkin
Alison Lawrence
Andy Lawrence
Jimmy Leach
Emma Leaf-Grimshaw
Esmé Lee
Lia Leendertz
Carl & Debs Legge
Alison Levey
Laurie Lewis-Knoedler
liliancarroll liliancarroll
limeweed limeweed
Rachel Lindsay
Ray Linforth
Nicola Lippok
Caroline Lister
Jonathan Littlewood
Eleanor Lloyd
Sarah Lloyd
Emma Loisel
LolaLovelyBonesJones
Sam Lomas
Wendy Lord
Dianne Lowry
Lucy, Jack and Maggie
Lorna Lynch
Zoe Lynch

Fraser Macdonald
Jane Mackenzie
Honor Mackley-Ward
Angela Malone
James Mann
Angela Mannis
Claire Manzotti
Belinda Marks
Camila Marlier
Terence Marmot
Nicky Marshall
Steve Marshall
Colin Patrick Martin
Jane Martin
Lisa Martin
Melanie Martin
Robert Masding
Catherine Mason
Sarah Mather
Edwyn Matless
Jim & Mira Mattern
John Peter Maughan
Niamh McCabe
Peter & Roisin McCan
Angela McCann
Laura H. McCann
Jennifer McClelland
Shannon McConnell
Faith McCord
Rory McDonnell
Ron McKeating
Mark McKellier
Colleen McKenna
Sally McKenna
John & Rachael McLaughlin,
    Vermont, USA
Sierra McLeod
Jennifer McMullan
Laurie McNeill
Ella Mcs
David, Ruth, Holly,
    Rowan & Bryn Meek

Charlotte Michael
Patricia Michelson
Sophie Midgley
Sheri-Leigh Miles
Kim Millar
Petra Hoyer Millar
William Millar
Heather Miller
Sarah Mills
Kay Minchington
Davy Mitchell
John Mitchinson
Deena Mobbs
Jos Mol
Amanda Molden
Malc Mollart
Michelle Molloy
Richard Montagu
Kole Morgan
Helen Morley
Duncan Morris
Sarah Morris
Sean Morris
Rich Mortimer
Saira Mortimer
Rebecca Morton
Tabitha Morton
Lucy and Julian Moss
David Mottershead
Nick Moyle
Lady Muck
Emma Mullins
Judy Munday
Hedvig Murray
Alice Myers
Sue Nagle
Mary Nally
Carlo Navato
Chris Neale
Lindy Neave
Aine Neville

Maisie Nevin,
  Daddy loves you
Patrick New
Sam Newell
Verity Newman
June Nicholls
Glenda Nielsen
Carolyn Nisbet
Emily Nolan
Sarah Norcliffe
Jo Norcup
Sandra Norder
Scarlett Nunn
Andrew O'Brien
Susan O'Donnell
Jenny O'Gorman
Lisa O'Malley
L-J O'Neill
Mark O'Neill
Derrie O'Sullivan
Gregory Olver
Linzy Outtrim
Philippa Oval
Amy Overy
Penny Owen
Kayhan Ozturk
Ingrid Paige
Jeremy Paige
Kathryn and Martin Palfrey
Alistair Parker
Guy Parker
Helen Parkins
Rosamund Parnell
Dave Parsons
Alexander Pascoe
Adrian Passmore
Philip Passmore
Jerome Payne
Stanislaw & Stefania Pazucha
Amy Pearce
Jorgen Pedersen
Karla Pemberton

Mali Perdeaux
Jane Perrone
Lorraine Perry
Lynne Perry
Mike Perry
Charlotte Petts
Wendy Pillar
Jane Elizabeth Plowright
Lana Poll
Justin Pollard
Julieanne Porter
Katherine Potsides
Erin Power
Jake Price
Sheila Price
Jan Pritchard
Emma Probst
Adam Proehl
Andrew Przewieslik
Kaisa Puustinen
Andrew, Eva, Aiden,
  Elise and Alexa Rankin
John Rankin
Simon Rankin
Virginia Rankin
Jennie Ransome
Julie Ratcliffe
Adele Ray
Juliet Rayment
Peter Rayner
Saima Razzaq
Stephen Read ~ Reads Nursery
Fiona Reece
Steven Scott Rennison
Karen Retra
Muna Reyal
Michael Richards
Barbara Rickwood
Hannah Roberts
Juliet Roberts
Caroline Robinson
Enid Robinson

Jayne Robinson
Kevin Robinson
Rachael Robinson
Sue Robinson
Lisa Rodgers
Miriam Rodway
Iain Rousham
Mandana Ruane
Vivian Russell
Fintan Ryan
Sally Ryder
Naomi Sackett
Sarah Salway
Christoph Sander
Clare Savage
Hannah Schlotter
Birgit Schmidt
Melanie Scott
Sui Kee Searle
Geoffrey Severn
Emma Seward
David Shaw
Andrew Shead
Amy Shelton Honeyscribe
Michael Sherrod
Juliet Shield
Lynn Shouls
Rebecca Sickinger
Holly Silvester
Claire Simpson
Donna Simpson
Alison Sims
Nanne Sinclair
Hannah Sked
Kate, Laura, Walter &
  Franklin Slegg-Newton
Cally Smart
Douglas Smith
Fintan Smith
Fiona Smith
Mark Ridsdill Smith
Sandra Smith

Sharon Julie Smith
Amanda Smotherman
Ray Smyth
Snow
Kelly Soper
Katharine Sorensen
Natalie Sowden
Lorraine Spark
Joanne Spittler
Daniel Spokes
Denis St George
Jennifer Stackhouse
Kate Stancliffe
Annie Stanford
David Stapley
Di Stapley
Clive Stevenson
Janet Stewart
Adrian Stockdale
Pia Støvring
Ed Sturley
David Suff
Antonia Sullivan
Annie Sutcliffe
Simon Suter
Rachel Swingewood
Michael Tait
Molly Tait-Hyland
Martin Talks
Karen Tanguy
Christine Tansey
James R D Taplin
Friend of Teal
Trina Thirlwell
Elizabeth Thomas
Adam Thompson
Libby Thompson
Patricia Thompson
Poppy Janet Elizabeth
   Thornton
Christian Tillmanns
Beth Tilston

Kathryn Tomlinson
Rachel Topps
Beverley Treece
Ann Trevorrow
Robert Triggs
Maud Truesdale
Clive & Margaret Turner
Karen Twible
Joanne Upton
Barbara Urbanic
Marijke Jose van der Laan
Nikki Vane & Mike Cornfield
Karin Vermeulen
Linda Verstraten &
   Pyter Wagenaar
Eloise Vestberg
Rosie Waites
Jackie Wales
John Walker
Laura Wall
Ciaran Walsh
Katherine Walton-Elliott
Philip Ward
Caroline Ward &
   Erinma Ochu
Sara Ward, Hen Corner
Annabel Wardrop
Elizabeth (Liz) Ware
Lorraine & Arthur Warman
Sara Watkin
Vicky Watkins-Ball
Denis Waugh
Tanya Weaver
Torsie Webb
Andrea Weber
Deborah Weber
Louise Welch
Stephanie Wells
Kat Whelan
Chuck Whelon
Jo & Steve Whiley-Morton

Whittington and Fisherwick
   Environment Group
Sally Wilkins
Lynn Wilkinson
Jeff Willans
Shona Williams
Patricia Willis
Sara Willman
Kendra Wilson
Charlie Winton
Annette Witte
Alexandra Wood
Helen Wood
Elizabeth Woodhead
Martha Worsching
Colin & Rachel Wright
Kenneth Wright
Murray Yeomans
Bob Young